The Organized Pastor

The Organized Pastor

Systems to Care for People Well

Doug Serven

White Blackbird
BOOKS

Published by White Blackbird Books, an imprint of Storied Communications.

Julie Serven edited the publication.
Sean Benesh designed the cover.

Printed in the United States of America.

ISBN: 13: 978-0-9973984-2-7

About White Blackbird Books

White blackbirds are extremely rare, but they are real. They are blackbirds that have turned white over the years as their feathers have come in and out over and over again. They are a redemptive picture of something you would never expect to see but that has slowly come into existence over time.

There is plenty of hurt and brokenness in the world. There is the hopelessness that comes in the midst of lost jobs, lost health, lost homes, lost marriages, lost children, lost parents, lost dreams, loss.

But there also are many white blackbirds. There are healed marriages, children who come home, friends who are reconciled. There are hurts healed, children fostered and adopted, communities restored. Some would call these events entirely natural, but really they are unexpected miracles.

The books in this series are not commentaries, nor are they crammed with unique insights. They are a collage of biblical truth applied to current times and places. The authors share their poverty and trust the Lord to use their words to strengthen and encourage his people.

May this series help you in your quest to know Christ as he is found in the Gospel through the Scriptures. May you look for and even expect the rare white blackbirds of God's redemption through Christ in your midst. May you be thankful when you look down and see your feathers have turned. May you also rejoice when you see that others have been unexpectedly transformed by Jesus.

Other books in the White Blackbird Book series include:

Heal Us, Emmanuel: A Call for Racial Reconciliation, Representation, and Unity in the Church
Everything Is Meaningless? Ecclesiastes
Birth of Joy: Philippians

Praise for The Organized Pastor

A helpful primer on organizational leadership for pastors. It was especially helpful from a church planting perspective. Brief, but loaded with helpful lessons and suggestions. All around great little book.

Rev. Nathan Shaver, Christ Community Church

Doug Serven gives practical advice for pastors who struggle to keep on top of multiple projects and roots this advice in the Gospel. You could read it an afternoon, but if you unpack the content it will improve not just your personal organization habits but also the effectiveness of your ministry.

Rev. Bryce Hales, Resurrection Orange County

Doug's thoughts, wisdom, experience, and transparency helped me get clarity, take responsibility, and see what needs to happen next to not only survive but keep moving our church in the right direction.

Rev. Chris Gensheer, Christ Church Mansfield

I'd like to dedicate and thank all those who have suffered through my incredible lack of organization!

Most especially my best friend Julie Serven, who has been through it all with me. She reminds me of who I am and what I'm called to be. I love you.

Thanks to my friends, colaborers, and mentors, to Bobby, Smitty, Jason, and the pastors in Oklahoma City, the Presbyterian Church in America, and Reformed University Fellowship, who have taught me so much.

Thanks to those who worked with and underneath me as I heaped on expectations without much clarity, especially my OURUF interns: John, Jonathan, Brittany, Anna, Ben, and Natalie. And my students who so often just had to hang in there as I figured this out.

Thanks to those who work with me now to love God, love people, and love the city in Oklahoma City with City Pres. I love working with you in this awesome church. Now you get to suffer through my next steps of organization. Thanks for your patience!

Thanks to those who helped me with this book, especially Julie, Jonathan, Beau, Dan, and Jason. Thanks to those who taught me all the things I'm passing along in this book. Sometimes I was listening.

I'm sorry to all those I stood up throughout the years because I wasn't an organized person or pastor. Please forgive me. Truly.

Table of Contents

Introduction

I stood up the former mayor of Oklahoma City.

Twice.

I had agreed to start a new congregation of the Presbyterian Church in America in Oklahoma City. I'd been a campus minister for ten years at the nearby University of Oklahoma, so I was familiar with the area and able to buzz up to the city every day. I knew that in the beginning stages of our new church—called City Pres—I needed to meet as many people as possible for networking and city investigation. That's what I was trying to do.

This former mayor had been immensely popular and had seen the city through tremendous growth. I felt fortunate to set up a meeting with him.

I showed up at our agreed-upon location for our appointment. I waited. I waited for an hour. The restaurant didn't have Internet (boo!), and I didn't want to pull out my computer anyway because I didn't want him to walk up on me working. People make mistakes, and I wanted to give him grace and cut him some slack. I wondered if he had written down the wrong time and had gotten there early. It happens. I'm a forgiving person, and I was thinking that not everyone is as organized as I am. But eventually I realized the mayor wasn't going to show up.

I finally left and returned to the coffee shop to check my email. He said he was sorry he'd missed me but had been there for thirty minutes.

Uh....

I went back over our email thread. I realized I'd blown it. For some reason I had written down the appointment an hour later than what he had said in his message to me. Why had I done that? It was completely in every way my fault.

I felt terrible. I was embarrassed and asked him if he would be willing to try again. I told him to pick any time he wanted.

He said a date, and I agreed to it no questions asked.

That's when I stood him up the second time.

It turns out that he picked our move week. It wasn't a big move—only thirty minutes north from Norman to Oklahoma City. We'd been in our house in Norman for ten years, and I have four kids, so it was going to be a beast.

I had cleared off the whole week so we could get established in our new house. The mayor's meeting was now the only appointment I had that week, so when I made it, I thought I would never ever forget it.

Except that my brain told me, "You don't have any appointments this week! You cleared it off! You're good to go." So I didn't look at my calendar.

And thus, I missed the appointment and thereby blew off the mayor twice.

That's not good.

He's since forgiven me. At least he says he has. But I'm not asking him for any more meetings.

So in one sense—it happens. We all do this sometimes. I don't really miss that many appointments. However, I have to admit that I did last week!

My buddy Lance has a ministry called Hope Is Alive. He used to be a prescription drug addict, which eventually led him into a lost and broken world. After a long time of barely managing, he ruined it all. He's recovered and come out of it, and now he calls himself a Hope Dealer. I love that, and I love meeting with him. It's always honest and encouraging, and I love to help his ministry because his ministry helps me and members of our church.

But I left him hanging at the coffee shop, because after I agreed to meet up with him I didn't put it on my calendar. Lance graciously forgave me when I apologized to him afterwards. But it absolutely stinks that I did that to him.

It happens. But—why does this happen?

There can be such a disconnect from my plans and communications to my calendar and schedule. And when I do that, I hurt people. I waste their time. I wasted the mayor's time. I wasted my friend Lance's time. I don't care enough or can't get it together to do the right thing.

I can make excuses, and people understand we make mistakes. These aren't the worst problems in the world. But in another real life way, it's just plain wrong.

I need to change. I shouldn't do that to people, and I need to figure out how not to.

The mayor probably is stood up all the time even though he's an important person. He's had so many meetings in his life that it's bound to happen. We didn't have anything earth-shattering to talk about, so if we missed that meeting it wasn't a huge problem.

But sometimes it's going to be someone who isn't as accommodating. Or it's someone who wanted to talk about something deep, something meaningful, and then I wasn't there. Or you weren't there. And we missed out. People will forgive us, but we didn't treat them with love and respect. We didn't value their time.

Jesus says we should love our neighbor as ourselves. We should love other people, even the least of these. We should love as he loved. We should honor people and their time. I'm not sure how he did it, but he was very purposeful in his days, in his time with people. He didn't succumb to the tyranny of the urgent. He wasn't a bumbling manager, nor a hard-charging executive. He was a prophet, priest, and king who cared.

I want to be like Jesus in this area, but struggle because I'm not naturally organized. I used to compensate for this by keeping my task list really small and at least implicitly asking people to cut me a ton of slack. On the Myers-Briggs test I'm an ENFP. That's the personality profile of an entrepreneur and schmoozer. I'm an ideas guy. I love vision. I love to brainstorm.

I hate lists! I stink at organization.

But I hate treating people poorly more than I hate lists. My ministry eventually grew large enough that something had to change in order for me to be faithful in caring for the people God had put in my path. I couldn't keep treating people the way I had. Not if I cared about the Gospel expanding and the church growing and people finding grace and mercy through the life and ministry God had given me.

This book is born out of many conversations I've had with pastors and church planters who want and need help. I realized, for whatever reason, people were calling me to talk about organizational leadership.

Huh. I'd been working on it for awhile, so I suppose people were seeing and noticing the difference.

Some pastors are eager to change. Some are reluctant. Some need it and know it. Some don't think they do. As I've talked with pastors, what you'll read about in the following pages are the recurring themes, advice, and best practices that kept coming up in our phone calls, meetings, and consultations.

Only you can do the work to change. This book is meant to be a help to you. I want it to be both inspirational and practical. I'm trying to keep it short, because I know you're busy. You don't want to and just honestly can't read hundreds of pages about organization.

If something isn't helpful to you, move on. You don't have to do it the way I suggest. But think about it, and if that helps you figure out the way you can do it better, then great! Sometimes we have to get to Plan B. You can only do that by figuring out that Plan A isn't working. Is your Plan A working? Do you have a Plan B yet? I may be overeager at times. Feel free to take my advice with a grain of salt. Smooth it over. Let go what isn't going to work for you.

In the end, I think being a pastor is one of the greatest things you could ever do. I love the church and believe in it. I think we need stronger, better, healthier pastors. That means you need to succeed (as God defines it, not as the world does) in what God wants you to do. I don't want you to be snowed under or feeling guilty all the time, and especially not by more suggestions in this book.

I know people don't understand what you do as a pastor. It's a tough, tough job. But you have been called and empowered and equipped to love even a misunderstanding people. Let's do the best job we can as we walk together with Jesus and hold out the words of life. Let's love and care well for God's glory and the good of Christ and his church.

Like I said, I'm not naturally "this way." I'm not an organized person. I had to ask for help and learn it because I wanted to get more done than I was doing, and I also didn't want to quit and burn out.

It's not impossible. Grace comes from the outside. Let's work on it together and have a hopeful vision for what can be. You'll make mistakes, but you'll be able to see them and correct them and deal with them. Your anxiety should go down, and you'll be more of a resource to others instead of frantic, busy, worried, and stressed. I'm not saying you'll get into some Zen-like trance. You're still a pastor. But you should be able to see how you need to deal with what's coming up and what you need to do, what God has called you to do. You should be able to tackle more by grace, and go home and sleep better. You'll still disappoint people, but you're not a disappointment.

God loves you, and he wants the best for you. I really believe that. He has you in this tough place with this tough calling because it's the greatest thing you can do to serve people. Let's serve them and care for them the best we can.

And let's try not to stiff the mayors of our cities. Or anyone else, for that matter.

Chapter 1

Your Time

I hope I don't have to convince you of how valuable your time is.

You only have so much time each week to get done what you need to get done. This is your biggest asset for accomplishing your tasks. Whether you have a staff of a dozen or it's just you at the office each week, you need to be thoughtful and efficient with your time. You need a plan and a system in order to be able to get things done and know what you have to let go.

This efficient use of time and systems is actually biblical. Some of us think we're more godly and pastoral if we never track or plan our time. That is false.

Think back to Moses in the Old Testament books of Exodus and Numbers. By God's direction and grace, he led out God's people from bondage and slavery. This is a story of magnificence and magnitude. The plagues! The rescue! The Red Sea! The Egyptians!

In addition to the dramatic stories of rescue, it is also a story of plans and systems. People still had to eat. They had to set up camp and get it together for a transient, moveable society. They needed order and laws. They needed arbitration and counseling. One of my engineering church members tried to figure out the volume of water it would take to hydrate this wandering tribe of thousands of people—it's astounding to consider the management this would take.

Moses tried to do it all, just like you would have. But in Exodus 18 we read that his father-in-law Jethro told him that it couldn't work that way. Jethro asked Moses why he was doing it all himself, and Moses rationally explained it to him. But Jethro pushed back. He said, *"What you are doing is not good. You and the people will certainly wear yourselves out, for the thing is too heavy for you. You are not able to do it alone"* (Exodus 18).

Jethro told him he had to delegate. He had to set up a better system in order to maximize what everyone was supposed to do, so that things could best work for God's glory and the good of the people. The leader had to lead and that first meant he had to give up trying to do everything.

We see the same thing in Acts 6. The disciples were doing it all. There were complaints about how people fell through the cracks. So they set up deacons in order to best care for the people. They needed a better system to pastor and help people. They needed to use their gifts and talents better.

You can't do it all. I can't. Let's get over it. All of us have to do things we don't like doing or don't want to do. I'm not suggesting you fix your schedule so you get to only do what you like to do 100 percent of the time. That's impossible and impractical and not pastoral ministry or real life. You can't do what you want to do all the time.

However, I am saying—you are in charge of your schedule and time. You actually do get to do what you want to do. Right?

Almost every pastor has the luxury of setting his or her own schedule. You forget that's true. You think you don't, but you actually do get to set it. You get to manage your day, week, month, and year. But you still complain.

Let's take ownership and get this right, so we can look back and say we did the best we could, and we can rest in God's providence for us. We can know that we weren't tossed around on the waves of life and circumstances. We need to have an anchor of hope that gives us surety and a humble confidence that we followed God today, this week, this month.

I'm one of the complainers. In fact, I used to be the chief complainer. I had too many things to do. I had too many people to meet. I felt overwhelmed all the time, and I went home exhausted and distracted. I couldn't get a handle on it. Remember: I'm disorganized by nature. My default is to let things come to me, and then I feel like I'm justified in not getting other things done. I still do this. It's really a discipline for me not to keep living life this way all the time every day and then complain about it all the way through as a victim.

In one of those normal weeks of normal life as I'd constructed it, a friend and mentor gave me a framed picture that I have on my desk. It says, "Everything changed the day I realized I had just enough time to get done the important things that had to get done." I try to look at that every day. It's not in the Bible, but it still haunts me in a good way. I saw myself.

Things did change for me. Not completely. Not utterly. I'm still an ENFP, so I have to fight against my tendencies and proclivities.

I hope they will change for you in a good way, too. I was forty-one when I realized I had to change. I realized I was in charge of my day. Of course, most days I give away my time and my heart to others. But that was and is by choice, and I want to be glad I did it. I sit with people and listen to them and cry with them, but that's by choice and I'm glad I do it. I can also say no. I can also and must get away in silence in order to pray. I can attend meetings and conferences and prayer retreats that nourish my soul. I can take my time and energy to God, instead of blaming others.

I answer some emails, and I don't answer others. I take meetings and say no to others. I go work out at the CrossFit 405 gym in the afternoons, and that means I have to miss some chances and opportunities. I am interrupt-able. I have margins. And I have boundaries. And I make mistakes. And I come home wiped out and spent. And I have to reevaluate my schedule, time, and priorities.

Ultimately, it's my week before God. It's my week before God to keep or give away or stay frantic or feel calm. It's my week to work until the last second or to have a plan that works 90 percent of the time and that I feel good about. It's my month and my year. I can plan a prayer retreat, a conference I'd like to attend, a day off, and a lunch by myself.

It's not my wife's fault or my staff's fault or my presbytery's fault or my church members' fault that I can't get things done. To semi-quote Michael Jackson, I need to look at the man in the mirror, and I need to make that change. Or I can go on being frustrated at everyone all the time.

Enough of that.

You have just enough time to get done what you are called to do. How can you do that?

You need a system.

Your Calendar

The basic Number One most foundational building block of all this organization is your calendar. Every calendar is a record of what has happened and also a future plan of what you think will happen or what you want to have happen. It's a vision for the future.

You should be able to look at your last full month by way of looking at your calendar. It may be on your computer, or it may be on paper as a daily planner. You should get it and look through it. How did you spend your time last month?

Look for patterns and cycles. Look for where you get frustrated or where you feel the most at rest and the most joy. What did you leave undone? Why? What waited until the last second? Why was that true? What was your favorite thing you did over that time?

Now think ahead for a few months. Not the month you're in right now, since you're already embedded in it. Look at two months from now.

What would that month look like if it were perfect? What would you get done? Perfect doesn't mean you are sitting on the beach and drinking margaritas. You would still get the tough stuff done. You would still have difficult meetings and hard conversations. But you'd feel good about it. You'd feel like you did what you were supposed to do, like you accomplished your job and calling.

So, how could you have that week, that month? Let's take a look.

Your Perfect Week

It may be easiest to print off a hard-copy calendar for this project. That way you can erase and see it in a tactile way. Print one off for each week a few months away from now. Or load up your Google calendar or iCal or whatever calendar you use.

Knowns. Next fill in your "knowns." These are your recurring meetings, your staff meetings, your have-tos. I have a staff meeting on Wednesdays at 1:30 p.m., so that goes on there. You may have a standing lunch or breakfast. Or a finance team meeting on the first Monday at 7 p.m.

I have learned that I need to work out every day, preferably at 4:30 p.m. That has taken me a long time to realize and then to get on the calendar as a priority that is non-negotiable! I used to be much more erratic, but I've learned I'm not a good pastor by late afternoon. I can't focus, and I go home tired and worn out, or else I'll go to the pub and try to forget about all the crazy conversations I had that day or week. I need to work out instead. So that has to go on the calendar. I need to have it on there so I can say no to people when they ask for that time (unless of course it's an emergency—which it seldom is).

Get all those knowns on there first so you can work around them.

Day off. Now, what about your day off? That needs to be weekly, and it needs to be on your calendar. We'll talk about that more later, but for now let's just get it on there. I take Fridays off. I feel like I need to get right back to work on Monday after my Sunday. If I take off Monday, then I think about Sunday too much. Friday works for me, but it means I have a lot I have to get done the other days of the week.

But I have Friday free. I try my hardest not to book appointments on Fridays, which honestly sometimes is nearly impossible. But it is possible if I just say no and schedule people for a different day.

Regular big tasks. The other big block of time that you need is when you do the stuff that isn't an appointment but has to get done. For me that big block is sermon writing. Since I preach 75 percent of the time at our church, I have about 40 weeks of the year when I need to have a sermon. I always write a full manuscript, so that takes time.

I need to be able to study, take notes, write my sermon, compile my preaching notes, and give it a practice go around. I never ever want to be cramming this at the last second. That's not the life I want to live. I have made it my practice to be done with plenty of time to spare because honestly I have other things to be thinking about Saturday night and Sunday morning. I need to be at my best, not scrambling to make it to the pulpit with something I've stayed up late trying to get together. The Holy Spirit really can speak to me on Thursdays and not Sundays at 3 a.m.

If you are preaching, then when do you write your sermons? If you're not writing sermons but have something else, then when do you do that? When do you write your Bible studies, or study your finance reports, or do that large chunk of your job where you need focused time? When do you do the thing that you're responsible for and that takes regular time?

I've found I do best in the mornings or early afternoons. It takes me ten to twelve hours a week to get my sermon together. So I need to have that time blocked off, and I need to be unavailable. It doesn't always work that way, but I try. It's important that I have an idea at least of when I'm going to work on this and also by when I'm going to be finished. Of course, some weeks go better than others. Some sermons come more easily, and some are rough last-minute stabs. Some weeks the wheels of the church fall off and every husband confesses his pornography addiction to his wife, and I can't control when that's going to happen. Some weeks I have no appointments, and it's like I'm the pastor of a ghost town where no one needs me.

But I need a baseline, to try to get a rhythm and pace that isn't crazy. I need to know what I'm aiming for.

So when are you getting these big things done? Do you have your knowns and your big weekly tasks down on your calendar?

Regular small tasks. You need to also have your other deadlines on your calendar. These are smaller things that get done each week or month. We'll talk more about those to-do lists and organizing them, but for now you need to have them in mind at least.

Things like:

- Welcome email to new visitors each Monday
- Expense report first day of each new month

- Agenda submitted a week before each finance team meeting
- Monthly/weekly communication, newsletter, email
- Etc.

You may have one hundred of these small tasks, the ones you do every week or month. Put them on the calendar so you can come to them and accomplish them. Set them up for a recurring event on your calendar and really try to get them done when they show up. If you know how long those tasks take and when you can most easily do them, then go ahead and put them down for a particular time each week. Or you might group them together and have "Office Work," for example, each Monday from 8 to 10 a.m. Then write in there what you're wanting to accomplish each week during that time block, so those things can get done.

People. The last big thing is people. You should have an idea of how many people you can meet with each week before you get nasty and cranky. You may have a large capacity or small capacity. God calls both introverts and extroverts into the pastorate. He wants us to extend ourselves but not to burn out and hate people. We need to have a mix of getting out there and spending time with people to live life together, but also to be spending time with God. We don't want to overextend ourselves, nor do we want to hide out in our offices and then wonder why people don't feel like they can talk to us.

You should know whether you can meet with about five people a week or ten or fifteen. Then you can see when those meetings best occur (if you could do whatever you wanted in your perfect week) and get those time slots on the calendar. It certainly doesn't always work out that way, but you should know what your best week looks like and what you'd like people to do. You can also tell if you have way too many people in a certain week and need to make some changes to accommodate that, or if you need to say no and postpone a few meetings to a better time for you if possible.

So when and how do you meet people? How do you set up your appointments? How do you determine when those slots are?

I think you should have at least an idea of those available time slots and then communicate them to people so they know where and when you usually meet with people. There should be a mix between what is most convenient for you and what also helps accommodate the regular schedules of those in your church.

Not everyone can make it to your office at 10 a.m. But you could meet them for 45 minutes at the closest Starbucks to their home or office. You could try to string together three or four of those appointments at the same place on the same day of the week by having that be where you go and inviting people to join you there. You could go to their office or work and then meet for lunch (as long as you factor in the travel time).

So now imagine you have laid out your perfect week. You meet with the right amount of people each week. You have your meetings that you're prepared for. You have your tasks accomplished. You have your down time in the correct places.

How do you feel about your week and about your schedule?

Your Year

Take that concept over the next full calendar year. Think about your vacation and when that will be and put that down. (If you don't have vacations written down, then we need to talk! You have to have rest built into your yearly schedule.) Think about a conference you'd like to attend and put that down. If you have regional or national meetings, then add those. Write down your regular events in the life of your church—look over your recurring conferences or when your week is erratic because of VBS or you know you have extra work to do because of Holy Week. You can know when those are.

You can write down the football games if you're in a college town. We never ever tried to plan anything when Oklahoma played Texas. It would never have worked since everyone was in Dallas at the game (and we wanted to watch). You can know when your city's festivals are and then join in because you anticipated that in your calendar.

I also propose you think through your year's sermons and have those all laid out. You could easily do that in December. Get some time away at a hotel in town and do a planning retreat. Buy the next year's calendar at the office supply store and get some markers and start filling in the year.

You can know when Easter is and thus when Lent starts. You can know when Super Bowl Sunday is. You can know that you can't bunch everything up in one or two weekends, so the men's retreat and the women's retreat can't be right after each other.

When I was a campus minister (and it's still true to some degree now), August and September were super crazy months. Even though school started near the end of August, there were a million back-to-school events, move-ins, meet and greets, and training times to gear up for. I had long days in Sam's Club to buy all the supplies. I had to almost instantly follow up on every new student contact before their attention went elsewhere. The campus had its own events that I needed to work around, and we had football games and sweaty tailgate parties to consider.

By October, I was wasted. I was spent. I was exhausted. I'd done all of that in the worst of the heat with the most pressure.

We all planned on busting our tails every August and September, but we knew we had to let off the gas in October. We couldn't sustain that pace. We had to plan for August, and we had to go through August, but we couldn't keep living that way. Such is the life of a campus minister.

Pastoring a church has different rhythms. People don't all move in one week. It's far more spread out. But you do have rhythms. You do have busier and less busy times. You do have seasons of intensity and distraction and focus. Right? You need to know when those are and that only comes when you have time to get away and think about your year, get things on the calendar and know they're coming. You can always make adjustments, and things never go quite as you planned, but you need to have a plan.

Do you have a plan?

Can you get an appointment on your calendar so you can see whether there is a conflict? Can you include the space you need to get other things done? Do you have margins in your days and weeks so when something unexpected happens, you know you have the makeup room to jiggle around time so you won't be crazy busy stressed?

What's it going to take to get there?

Action Steps:

- Pray about your schedule, your time, your outlook, and your demeanor. Ask God to help you see what he wants you to do and where you best live life to serve and love him and people well.
- Investigate some best practices for calendars. Buy a program or an app that gets good reviews. If you don't like it after giving it a good try, then move on and see whether something else works better for you.
- Interview someone who seems to have a good handle on time and doesn't appear to be harried, overwhelmed, and too busy. Ask him or her three or four things, and then try those things.
- Try a scheduler program like ScheduleOnce.
- Take a picture of your week, your month, and your year and send it to me if you want help and interaction.
- For a hard-core book about time management, pick up the *No BS Time Management for Entrepreneurs*, by Dan Kennedy. His books are easy to read, no holds barred, and pretty funny. You can pick up some helpful ideas, even if your time isn't worth a literal $2000 an hour.
- Dream about your perfect week, month, and year and put it down on paper or on your computer. Then realize that you can make that happen.
- Plan a planning retreat.
- Write down your day off on your calendar and keep it clear.
- Figure out what you like to do for exercise and do it as much as you can.
- Read "Here's the Schedule Very Successful People Follow Every Day" at Time.com (July 2, 2014). Basically, their schedule looks like this:

1. Morning Ritual
2. Important Work First Thing—With No Distractions
3. Regroup When You Slow Down
4. Meetings, Calls, and Little Things in the Afternoon
5. A Relaxing Evening

Chapter 2

Your People

"My wife found out I've been looking at pornography. What should I do next?"

This is the start of a normal conversation that begins at the coffee shop where I usually meet people. This businessman husband tells me that he's confessed to his wife what he's been looking at or she found out and confronted him, and how he's scared and wondering what's next.

We sit, and we talk. We cry, and we try to hope together. He has a pit of shame in his stomach, but he is earnest and wants to stop viewing and lying. He hates himself. I try to press into him God's love and forgiveness for his children, to call him out of the shame and guilt and into the light of grace and truth.

But then we get to "Now what?" It's a long, complicated road ahead. There is rooted history here with him. That fact, that sin, has affected his wife for a long time, and she may not even know that it has. She's about to have a conversation that she doesn't want to have in any form or fashion. She's involved in every way, even though it's not her thing.

He can trace back stories that connect with other people. Stories of harm and hurt, of interest and involvement. He's going to have to start telling those stories to unravel the knots and see what forgiveness is going to look like.

He and I will install blockers on his computer so he can better (though not mechanically, perfectly) live in freedom and give himself and others space to heal and talk without being immersed in the thing itself. He needs to admit he needs those blockers and then install them and thus inflict some amount of rules and structure on his life. That will come at a cost and perhaps another conversation.

I have this meeting all the time. I'm glad to. I'm glad people are admitting to and coming out of such destructive addiction.

I know there will be subsequent meetings with his wife. She'll be shocked. Confused. Betrayed.

She'll wonder about the legitimacy of this marriage and his covenantal vows. She'll wonder about her life-long body issues, and this will tap into that incredible bruise that has been present for thirty-plus years. She'll remember the time she was abused or the times her friend or coach or teacher or parent or pastor implied (or explicitly stated) that she would be more or better accepted if she were _______ .

These conversations, though, are complicated because they involve not one person but many. A church is connected. Sins are not exactly private at all. They affect people, families, coworkers, spouses, friendships.

When you think about pastoring your people, you know that it's complicated. True pastoring isn't contained only in Monday Bible study breakfasts and set up and clean up. Or only in preaching and teaching. It's giving people the space and hearing to open up and confess that they truly need Christ in every way today and every day. It's offering Christ to them in hopeful tears.

Every person in your church has hundreds of relationships, and that only multiplies when you get a bigger and bigger church. When you think of pastoring your people, do you get overwhelmed or excited about how God is at work?

How big do you think your church should be? What is its ideal size?

It's a good question to ask yourself and even to ask other pastors. I don't think there is a correct answer to this question, but it's helpful to wonder about when you consider the givens you already have in place. Think about yourself and your capacity, your staff team, your building, your budget, the demographics of your town or city, the age and stage of life of your ministry. Now, how big do you think your church should be?

It may be 50 or 150 or 550 or 5000. Be realistic.

Behind each individual number is a person. And each one of those people has problems, issues, hopes, dreams, sins, and redemptive traits. And each one of those people has dozens of other people in relationship past, present, and future. (One book you might pick up on this theme is *Creating a Healthier Church*, by Ronald Richardson.) Thinking about this complexity of relationships can be overwhelming!

This complexity means you cannot track what every single person is doing every single moment. You can't pin down discipleship quite so easily. You can't get people through the program you've established and then think they're good to go.

It doesn't mean you can't have a system. I think you should have a system. But you can't rely on the system to pastor the people.

The system helps you get at pastoring them. It helps you help them to pastor each other. It needs to work and get people together and talk and then instill the values that you want to see so they can see Christ more fully in their brokenness as they're having conversations like the one I described at the beginning of the chapter. You want a way to be able to connect with people all along the need spectrum so you can help them when they need it. You want the church to truly be a place of belonging, challenge, and comfort at the right times.

How do you do that?

Visitors

Let's assume you have visitors. You should. How are you going to track those visitors so they might possibly become fully integrated members? That may take a long time, and it may involve many steps. Some visitors are cognizant (and vocal) about their reasons and wants for a new church. Others just show up and don't know what they're looking for.

You need to be able to know about them and interact with them so they can feel invited and welcomed to join your church body in its mission and vision. That means you need a system.

You need to be able to identify a visitor and then start to follow up with that person along the way. You should take very seriously this person and try to do everything you can to connect with him or her. That doesn't mean coddle or drop everything to make him or her happy. But it does mean that first impressions and communications are essential and worth figuring out. Some people want to be left alone. People don't want to be pressured and smothered, but they do want to be seen and noticed and invited into the discussion.

You should interview people at churches that have a great reputation with visitors. As a baseline, do what they do. Just take their system and try to make it yours to whatever extent is possible. An organized pastor makes use of what other people have figured out how to do well and then freely gives credit where it is due.

Somehow then you need to identify those visitors and get their information. We have tear-out sheets that get placed in the offering basket. We love it when visitors are willing to share their email addresses. It's tough for us to track with someone until that key step happens. Not everyone is willing to give it out quickly, which is understandable and fine. We don't make anyone. We don't cajole people. We invite them onto our Wednesday weekly email, where we deliver special content and announcements.

But that's not all. Many churches stop there. I think an organized pastor would send a personal email or letter or note to each person upon getting that information for the first time.

Mine goes like this:

There are a lot of reasons people might visit a new church, and I'd love to hear what yours is. We're all telling our story of rescue, but it's not all figured out. We hope you'll join in with us as we walk together with Jesus.

We're trying to get started to really see what the Lord would do in our great city as we love God, love people, and love the city.

If you'd like to get together and talk, I'd love to get coffee with you—just let me know.

We hopefully have some good connection points with our CityGroups (these meet in homes throughout the city) and other ways to get involved.

We'd love to be your church home.

You can learn basic information about us at citypresokc.com. We often try to update daily life and some events through our Facebook page.

We best and most organize ourselves on The City: citypresokc.onthecity.org. This is the place where we try to be a real community, share prayer requests, and share our stories of rescue that aren't just for all the Internet to see.

I'll be sending you more emails throughout the year so I can tell you about City Pres. Simply unsubscribe from the list if you would prefer to not receive them.

I look forward to hearing from you!

Doug Serven
Pastor, City Presbyterian Church

I'm telling you this not because you have to do it this way, but so you can have an idea of the way I introduce myself and my church in a way that hopefully gives information and an invitation to more conversation and interaction. You may have a better email or better approach. You may make a personal visit—which means you have to have an address and the time. You may have a welcome basket—which means you have to make sure you haven't given one before and the person doesn't feel badgered.

What I'm suggesting is that you have a system of contact and then a way to track that person after that. Did you get an answer back? Did the person return a second time? What about follow-up emails giving more information about the church?

I have learned to enter this person into an automated program that then will email him or her every few weeks with a bit more information and contact. These subsequent emails will go out automatically whenever I start them. They talk about different ministries in the church, the history of how we got there, what the Gospel of Christ is about, and ask and answer common questions.

Will it work? I don't know. I do know that this is a system of communication and care and a way to track those who are at least "in" enough to give us their information. It's not a substitute in any way for preaching, teaching, great music, strong friendship, and warm greetings. Studies show that people care a lot about clearly marked signage, a great nursery, and good parking, too.

An organized pastor cares about integration and assimilation, and has a way to determine whether they're happening or not. (It's harder for him or her to do that when the sermon isn't done until the last second.) An organized pastor collects the data and then uses that with even more warm greetings and interactions, all to enhance the idea that we would love to have them as part of our church, involved with our unique vision and mission.

It's tough to be organized with people you don't know yet. You need to be able to find them, meet them, and then help them. You need to be able to introduce them to others in your church in order to enhance their relationships so they can thrive and grow and help you. That's caring for people.

Your Church

Let's say a family or person does track all the way to membership. They're now regular attenders. They're giving. Their kids are involved in the kids and youth programs. The adults are in a small group/community group. They're serving at various times each month. Success!

But of course their life is more complicated than that surface view gives. One of the kids struggles with school. Another of the kids is so shy that the family can't try new things because this child is petrified of meeting new people. The husband is stressed at work and can't get out from under the pile. He has a grandfather who just passed away, and he can't make it to the funeral. She just had the conversation where he confessed his addiction, so her world is rocked. Now what?!

If it hasn't happened yet, it will happen. Families are complex, with people and sin and patterns of coping. So now you just got one of those family systems in your church. And because you are now that individual's or family's pastor, that has implications for how you will be spending your time.

In Jeremiah, we read that the heart is deceitful above all things and beyond cure—who can understand it? I take that to mean that sin is really, really bad. It's not just sort of bad. It's bad. Gross. Terrible. Killer.

But Jesus says that he has come to make all things new. That he brings abundant life in him. That the wages of sin is death, but the gift of God is eternal life in Christ Jesus our Lord. We find truth and grace as we walk with him and uncover and discover our greater—not our lesser—need of him.

So that means we're on this journey together of finding Jesus to be even more beautiful and believable. That we're worshiping, serving, confessing, believing, hoping, creating, and thinking together.

We shouldn't be surprised when someone goes off the rails or finally realizes something in a new way. In fact, we should expect it. That's what walking with Jesus looks like. We don't have it all together. We don't have it all figured out. That's not a free pass to just be idiots and jerks. It means that we are worse off than we thought, but that Jesus is also better than we thought.

I think the organized pastor realizes and recognizes this and takes it into account with his or her interactions with people. It's not like every week people suddenly realize how incredible and insightful your sermon was. It's more like one week the wheels fall off and you have a conversation that is exactly what you were talking about six weeks ago in the sermon about Esther—except this person wasn't listening. She was corralling her kids and wondering about how many calories are in balsamic vinaigrette and why is it so hot in here and I like her dress and wow they must be fighting and oh, I guess we're done....

But now she wants to talk. Fair enough. People need what they need when they think they need it.

The organized pastor tries to get at this through:

- Follow up
- Periodic emails and invitations to talk more
- Questions for interaction

I don't want to make it sound more complicated than it is. And I'm not trying to suggest that this will fix anything. It's not fixing. It's recognizing that people have problems at different points, and they're mostly reluctant to talk about them.

So after that couple has tracked all the way into membership, they are now in a new category of relationship with me and the church. If they had decided to leave the church and went somewhere else, I would graciously remove them from the list so they don't keep getting emails from me and the church.

Since they haven't, I don't want my communication to cease. I don't want them to think that I had put all of that time and energy into getting them in and now that they're members, I'm dropping them and moving on.

I need a plan.

My plan is that every six to seven months I send them an email. It doesn't take much. It is a variation on this:

> I hope you're having a great day and a great week. If there is anything at all that I can do for you or know about or pray about, I'd love to do that. Anything.
>
> I just wanted to say howdy and let you know that I was thinking about you.

Simple enough. No big deal. I have various ones so I don't send the same one over and over. I'll adjust it for the time of year and the number of interactions or the number of ignored responses.

What I've found is that most people really appreciate being prayed for and getting an email from the pastor. Most of the time there isn't anything special going on, and I don't get a dramatic response, which is fine by me. I'm not digging for something.

But sometimes I will get something deeper. I'll get an email about struggling with doubt and depression. I'll hear, "I've been cutting myself." Or "I need to talk." Or "I need a roommate and can't find a place to live." Or "My fiancé and I are calling off the engagement."

I get that because I asked. I asked because I had it down to ask because I care. I care because I'm the pastor. But I can't keep all these things straight just in my head. I need a system to help me.

Do you have a system to help you keep track? What is it? How do you manage the relationships that are building as your church grows and gets more complicated? You don't have to know every person, but does someone in the church know each person? Does every person in the church have someone that might ask this question even at random times?

I want our church to be one that cares and knows. I want us to send flowers when someone is sick or having a hard time. I want us to send a jerky-of-the-month to a dude who is struggling with recovering from a surgery. I want us to identify and then help those with needs that don't rise to the level that normally get help.

That means we have to be organized. Which is a tough job. But it's possible if we're organized pastors.

When we are efficient in our organization and communication, we can then enter into the inefficient life of pastoring well. People take time, and they don't come in neat little tidy packages. We have to go to the hospital and sit with the sick and dying. It's our privilege. We get to go and hold a baby an hour after it is born. We attend weddings and funerals. Weddings are planned far in advance, but funerals never come at a good time. We clear our days for family emergencies and interventions.

Because we care and because we know and because we walk together with people who need Jesus and in fact we need him ourselves.

People You Don't Know—Yet

I think one of the jobs of a pastor is to network with people. I'm not sure everyone would agree with me.

This isn't a huge part of our calling. It's not even close to the main part. But I do think it is in there, especially if you are starting a new church. We have to get out there and meet people.

I think the organized pastor considers this and then takes it seriously. He or she doesn't make this the only thing, because there are a million other things to do. And the wise pastor leverages each meeting and appointment to maximize the impact.

So how do you do that?

The first thing you have to do is get the long-term best mindset. When we talk about networking, we most often tend to think about what we get. It makes sense. You are trying to get people interested in and recommending and visiting your church. That's ultimately what you want.

Ah, but that is using people, and they're going to figure that out quickly. They're going to cringe when they see you coming. They're going to wish they hadn't seen you, and pretty soon your reputation is going to be that all you care about is growing your church (which may be true!).

What I'd like for you to consider is the parish pastor. That pastor is the one who knows everyone and wants the best for the city. The church is involved in that city. It's involved in the flourishing of the city and it being the best city it can be. When the city does well, it makes this pastor (hopefully you!) happy. When the city does poorly, it makes you the pastor sad. You celebrate and grieve with the city as it moves forward in all its ways.

There are certainly times when we're countercultural, and we're always remembering that our citizenship is ultimately in heaven. We're not so connected to the city that we can't critique it and speak against its idols. But we do so as insiders, as residents of that very city.

The key concept here comes from Jeremiah 29:7, which says, *"But seek the welfare of the city where I have sent you into exile, and pray to the Lord on its behalf, for in its welfare you will find your welfare."*

Since this isn't a theological book about Christ in culture (read Leslie Newbigin and Tim Keller), I won't go too much into this, although it's a passionate point for me. I want City Pres to grow and flourish, but City Pres is a congregation in the city of Oklahoma City. I need to pay attention to what is happening in my city. I need to read the newspaper. I need to know people. I need to spend time with very important people and those who are down and out. I need to—eventually at least—spend time at neighborhood meetings and hearing what people who care about my city are talking about. Because I'm one of those people!

So I think the organized pastor has at least a few things in his or her month that would show that that's true. She doesn't get obsessed with these meetings and think of herself as a socialite. She doesn't necessarily seek out every meeting or event possible. She doesn't neglect her church in order to be seen at the ball. She doesn't think that successful people are actually more important or better.

But she does look for ways to meet people and gain access to new insights, understanding, and ways to help people.

That's networking, right?

I think you should get involved in one or two things that you care about and enjoy but that also are ways for you to meet people that you wouldn't normally meet. I've recently become interested in city planning and development. That's been true since I moved to Oklahoma City and started City Pres. I started reading the paper and tracking with different neighborhoods and developments. I was invited to and joined something called ULI—Urban Land Institute. It's a way to meet other people interested in making Oklahoma City a better place. We have meetings where we get to tour new buildings going up. We have lunch and talk about Better Block and street patterns and new streetcar systems. I meet people, and they meet me.

When we bought a historic building for our church, some ULI friends asked if they could be one of the first to tour the building. So I set up a time where the local chapter came. We had beer and sandwiches. I asked the key players who put together the deal—all of whom were from ULI—to briefly talk about their roles in helping a church buy a building and why in the world they would help make that happen. I barely spoke at all. It was glorious.

I'm not saying be like me. I'm saying find that thing that's a bit outside of pastoring but is connected to caring for the city. The Rotary Club. The local college. The school board. The coffee shop crawl. The art promotions. Be organized and intentional, but also have fun and just be free to bless other people.

The truth is that very few people in your city will ever come to your church. It would be amazing if City Pres grew by a few hundred people in the next few years. But that is such a tiny percentage of people who live and work in Oklahoma City. Yet, still we care. We seek to bless people who will never come to our churches because we care about people.

When you network to bless others, you become someone who cares about others doing well. And that makes you someone that people like. The church has a huge reputation for using people. Let's bless people! Let's help them succeed in life, business, family, and more. So when you go to these events and meetings, you can be free to connect two people together so they succeed and you can get out of the way. You become an instigator. You become what Seth Godin calls a "linchpin." And it's tremendously fun.

I can almost guarantee (almost) that somewhere down the line this person is going to refer someone to your church. He's going to say, "I don't know what it is about Bob, and I've never been to his church, but you should check it out. They're really involved in the city, and they really love people and I've been impressed with what I've seen. Something different is happening there." Boom. That's huge.

That's not why you do it, but it will likely happen as a result. That's the way it works. Think of how you'd like to be treated, and try to treat others that way. Would you like your church to be recommended on social media? Would you like your church's events to be spread throughout the city and people to invite their friends to come who've never been? Then perhaps you should treat someone else like that. Promote their fundraiser, their event, their gala, their meeting, and then show up and bring someone and introduce him to someone he needs to know. It will come around.

Collect those emails. Get those contacts. Then have a plan to follow up with these people in your city. Carve out a few lunches per month to connect with people you've been meeting. Not to use as recruiting lunches. But to ask how they're doing and to take an interest in their life and business (just like you'd like for them to take an interest in you).

What's your plan? What's your organized strategy? How many meetings like this would you like to have each month? It may be one or two or five or whatever. But they're not just going to happen. Plan them out and then ask people to meet with you. Follow up with a thank you and then set it in your calendar to get back with them in six months.

One More Step of Networking

Let me talk about one other thing before I give you a practical step on how to organize this.

You have one other ring of contacts out there. This is the wider group of people who you have some sort of association with. They are:

- Your regional pastors
- Your friends from seminary
- Your contacts from past jobs and locations
- Friends who have moved away and now are all over the nation
- Your high school and college classmates
- Your family

I like to contact these people every so often, perhaps once a year. These are people that matter to me, but I don't often act like it. It's so easy to forget them and only respond when there is a big need. I've been trying to send a once-a-year howdy, a "How are you? We don't often get to talk, but your friendship is important to me. I'd like to know how I can pray for you and what I can know about that is going on in your life."

It's pretty simple. It's not a big deal. It doesn't take a lot of time.

The main reason I do this is because I actually do care, or at least I want to care. But I need an action step besides just saying I care. I need a way to show I care so that I can care. It's cool to get a response and have a conversation about how they're doing. Sometimes I can offer a bit of help or advice or point them to someone who can help. Sometimes.

And it's also true that sometimes I will need help from one of those people, but I don't know when. And sometimes they'll know of someone moving to Oklahoma City that is going to need a church.

My thought process is that if it's easy, then I could do it. So let's make it easy and then see what happens.

How Do You Do This?

I hope I've sufficiently covered the why for all of this: caring. Establishing contact. Being there when someone needs you. Helping others. Loving the city. Being a pastor in the city instead of using the city for yourself.

I'm guessing it might sound pretty overwhelming to keep track of all of this! It is. That's why my unorganized, natural self never could in a million years. I would think of these things and then just give myself a pass because they were impossible.

However, I have realized there are tools that help. There are other jobs that have this sort of contact management, and we can learn from them.

The one I use and the best one I've found is the one I want to tell you about. I'm sure there are others, and you should use the one that you like and makes sense for you.

I use Contactually. It's a Contact Resource Management (CRM) system. Its main use is for tracking contacts for sales. I've found that I like these types of business software solutions better than the so-called Christian ones. I think they make improvements faster and try to stay more relevant.

This isn't meant to be a huge commercial for Contactually per se. Use the system you like. There are others out there that help you get things done and care about people. But since Contactually is the one I use, I will tell you how I use it, and then you can see what you think.

It's connected to your email account, so mine is linked to my Gmail account, and it pulls contact info from there. It also can track your other accounts like Facebook and LinkedIn, whatever you direct it to use.

The biggest thing to understand is that you then have to sort your contacts into buckets. Each bucket can have a name or title, and then you can give each bucket a frequency setting for how often you want to connect with and send an email to the people in that bucket.

So for me:

- New Contacts – every 60 days
- Church Members – every 120 days
- Oklahoma City Contacts – every 150 days
- Ministry Friends – once a year
- Friends and Family – every 270 days (just to keep it interesting!)

- No Need to Contact – a list where I put people I don't want to email
- Etc.

You can set up as many of these, and you can also have people in more than one bucket. You can have some buckets with very infrequent contact, if any.

One of the biggest tasks with something like this is always setting up the information on the front end. It can be overwhelming to get started. My suggestion is to power through a few sessions of maximum bucketing and then regularly keep at it with maintenance. It takes time and effort to be organized.

The next big thing is to set up some email templates. This is where you write the emails that you're going to send to the various buckets. I recommend giving these emails names that will both clearly say the topic or audience for the email as well as where it falls in the order of sending. You want to be sure that if you've sent Visitor Email #1 (Contactually will show what you have sent) that the next time you send Visitor Email #2 instead of (oops) Visitor Email #1 again. Contactually has email templates for you to use if you get stuck. The best thing is to just start using it and make adjustments as you figure out your system more.

Contactually has an incredible support team that will help you out with personal phone calls. There have been times I've gotten off track and out of the habit, and they helped me with some things I'd been doing that had been sabotaging my efforts. In the time on the phone, I also learned new things, so my efficiency and organization zoomed ahead even more.

Once you have these email templates set up, you're ready to go. I have my account set to email about eight to ten people per day. Each morning I open up Contactually and send those emails. The idea is that I make contact with various people in a caring, intentional way instead of only waiting for them to contact me with needs. It takes me five minutes or less. Sometimes I have to make a few adjustments to an email, but mostly I can zip these out in no time.

Five minutes to contact people and try to pray for them and help them? Sounds good!

I've been advocating this type of intentional approach throughout this chapter. I'm telling you something that makes it easier to be organized and connect with and care for people in your various circles of influence—visitors, members, those in your city, those in your world.

If you don't use this method, that's fine. I'd love to know what you use and how you do it. Like I said, I don't want this to distract from sermon writing and important church matters. If this took up a ton of time, I wouldn't do it. But I have found that it's pretty simple after getting it set up.

Here is what my friend Wes Martin says about Contactually. He started using it while he was in seminary after I told him about it:

> I have always struggled to keep up with my friends that I meet as I travel around. I'm a guy who meets a lot of people and genuinely cares for them, but it's just so hard to keep up with so many people. Contactually is a service that takes all of my contacts from my email, my phone, Facebook, and every other social contact thing I have and

puts them in one place and keeps track of whether or not I have talked to them.

I really do care about people, and I hope the fact that I need a service doesn't mean that I'm a bad friend. But I really want to be a friend to a lot of people, and so Contactually has allowed me to really and genuinely touch base with people from time to time so that I can keep those relationships growing. Even in the first thirty days of using it, I have touched base with people I haven't talked to in years, and I think they really appreciated that I looked in with them and that will help our friendship keep growing, even if only a little bit of the time, for years to come!

Action Steps:

- What type of involved and organized pastor do you want to be? Ask God to show you how you can better care for the people he has brought you to know.
- Pick a CRM program that works for you. Consider Contactually. Sign up for a free month at a discount I've worked out for you by using the code "citypresokc." I have a webinar on the Contactually site specifically for pastors and church planters. They also have a good webinar on networking. Or figure out something else better and let me know what it is.
- Make time in your schedule for a few networking friendship lunches or meetings.
- Think about where your interests are. See whether there are any groups in your city that might help you in that area of interest. Join up with one or two of those groups.

Chapter 3

Your Church

I can tell you how to go from a church of zero to 250 in three years. I also can tell you how I raised $400,000 in six weeks so we could purchase a historic building in downtown Oklahoma City. I can tell you how to track and process membership.

I can tell you these stories, but although they may be dramatic and compelling, they are in some sense specific to me and to what God chose to do in Oklahoma City. We hit an incredible demographic at just the right time. I had been a campus minister for ten years at the state university down the road, so I knew a ton of graduates in the city who had never found a church home. I met someone who wrote a $300,000 check because he believed in what we were doing and wanted to help us complete the project we'd been working on. I didn't plan any of those things.

I certainly prayed for them. I didn't luck into them. They didn't "just happen." I worked my tail off to get things up and running so we could communicate our particular vision and invite people who were excited and available to join us. I tried to identify and then recruit people who had been underutilized and were willing to help us with sound systems, nursery setup, graphic design, and leadership. I showed up at places and tried to love people. I had an incredibly gifted friend who joined me so we had two pastors start our church from the very beginning.

You're not in this same situation. I think I can help you, but you're you, and I'm me (profound, I know). You have a particular demographic in your city and your church. You have your own personality and proclivities. We could work together to enhance your website, your communication, and your outreach. We could spend time talking about what you do that unintentionally detracts from people reaching out and inviting others. There are consultants that can help you, and I think you should use them. They're worth it.

Systems

However, this book is about organization for you as the pastor of a church. You're a leader. You're the leader.

You need systems to help you lead. Organization isn't about personality profiles or abilities. It's about recognizing like Jethro did for Moses that everyone needs systems in order to best lead more and more people. You can handle a small amount of people with almost any methods. But if you want to grow, then things will get more and more complex. You'll need systems to track that growth, that complication, that recurring problem, so you can devote yourself to more and better work, while making sure it all gets done like you want it to be, like it needs to be.

What I'd like for you to do is agree with me on this. Can you?

There are simple systems and complex ones. A simple system would be remembering how every year you make an announcement about the Super Bowl and what your church's plans are. No big deal, except you can forget. Forgetting isn't the end of the world, so the stakes aren't that high.

An effective, efficient system would be to put a note in your calendar (or your task management system, which we'll talk about later) on January 10 each year that pops up and says, "Make Super Bowl Announcement." You could attach last year's announcement to make it even easier. Now you don't have to remember. It's there, every year on repeat so it shows up and you can remember to make that announcement.

I'll bet you have hundreds of small things like that you could automate and get down on your calendar and out of your mind. We'll talk about some of them, but your brain is busy trying to retain them, sort them, and keep track of them. You burn valuable energy and brain functioning just in those small, regular tasks. A simple system gets them down and offloads them into something that is better at remembering—a computer.

A much more complex system might be tracking someone from a first-time visit to membership and then to giving for the first time. Our membership process includes watching videos, attending a class, doing a background check, filling out a membership packet that includes a testimony, having a face-to-face meeting with one of the pastors, completing a sexual abuse awareness training class online (called Ministry Safe, which we require in order to work in the nursery), and then showing up and taking the vows at church on a certain Sunday. Goodness gracious, that's a lot of steps!

So we need a way to keep track of all the things that need to happen, including scheduling those meetings and times, hosting the meeting, tracking people for what they've done and haven't done, and then even figuring out who is going to show up that membership Sunday to take the vows. What happens when people complete almost all of those steps but not all? How do we identify those who haven't done Ministry Safe training yet?

I could keep track of this myself when we had fifty people. But I knew that Bobby (my co-pastor) and I would soon be swamped. So we worked on developing systems.

For instance, one thing that drives me crazy is typos in the worship song slides. I understand how it happens. I create typos myself. It irks me when we have misspelled "judgement" with that extra "e" in there (this is a common mistake). Or when the worship team sings different words than what are on the screen or bulletin.

But what normally happens is I notice it, but then the slide changes and time passes, and we've all moved on. Then I'm preaching and we do the Lord's Supper, and I don't think about it again until the next time the slide shows up, which may be six months later. Argh! There's that slide again!

So I need a system to fix that slide. It's not just going to fix itself. What is the process for it to be identified, for the right person to be notified, and for that slide to get fixed? It's a tiny thing, but it happens all the time. Now the worship leader gets a text with the error, and he fixes it. I can't wait. I have to do it right then, even during the service. It's not a complex system, but it's one that he knows is in place, so he's not upset that he's getting a text. We both want the words to be correct.

Little things matter. They're important. We show we care when we notice and fix things that can be fixed. We should have our slides spelled correctly. We shouldn't have typos in our bulletins. We're saying this sheet of paper is extremely important for worship—but we can't spell words correctly or use punctuation in the right manner?

I'm ranting, I know. This upsets me. But I'm the one who made some of those typos! So I need a system to eradicate them. It needs to be a system that works and gets the job done, but doesn't oppress people or make them feel scrutinized. We all make mistakes. It's fine. But let's come up with a way to fix the mistakes when we see them instead of perpetuate them.

Enough. Are you with me? Do you have good systems?

Do you ever stop and think back about your systems and evaluate them?

Pastor Luke Simmons of Redemption Church in Phoenix, Arizona, suggests evaluating your systems in the following areas:

WORSHIP PLANNING

- Do you have an annual preaching calendar prepared?
- Have you fully implemented a day/time when all Sunday preparation is finished (the "Thursday Midnight" rule)?
- Do you have a weekly Sunday evaluation meeting with follow-up?
- What went right?
- What went wrong?
- What was confusing?
- What was missing?

WORSHIP SERVICE

- Does the "feel" of the worship experience appropriately communicate to your target people group?
- In what ways do you use insider language in leading worship, announcements, sermon, communion, etc.?
- How smooth are your transitions from each service element?
- Do you start and end the service on time?
- Does anything communicate to Christians that this would not be a good environment to invite their unchurched friends to attend?

EVANGELISM

- Do you have a clear, written new believer process?
- What do you want new believers to know and do in the first hour, week, and month?
- What is your plan to get them into a group?
- Do you have a plan in place for personal and staff accountability to build relationships with non-Christians and invite them to church?
- Do you have easy ways for people to invite friends to church (invite postcards, evites, etc.)?
- Do you have a plan for encouraging corporate missional engagement?

HOSPITALITY

- How is your signage? Do you have enough signs/ banners? Are they big enough? Clear enough?

Simple enough? Do your signs clearly indicate where the restrooms and the kids check-in are?
- What is the quality of your coffee and refreshments? Does it communicate generosity?
- Do your greeters and ushers take a proactive approach to ministry?
- How likely is it for a guest to be engaged in a conversation with somebody from the church?

ASSIMILATION

- Are you getting 70 percent or more connection card completion rate?
- Are you writing weekly, handwritten notes to first-time guests?
- Do you have a regular evaluation of your assimilation system, where you look at how people were greeted, directed, treated, and seated?
- What are your next-step percentages? What percentage of first-time guests come back for a second visit? What percentage of second-time guests attend a connection event? What percentage of people who attend a connection event plug into community or service?

GROUPS

- Do you have simple, one-step small group sign-ups? Is it easy for people to sign up for a group?
- Are the senior leaders personally involved in a group?
- Do you have clear, written expectations of group leaders?
- Do you have 60 percent or more involvement in groups?

KIDS

- Is your kids environment secure (no parents allowed in rooms, stickers with numbers, etc.)?
- Is it obvious who the teachers and volunteers are?
- How simple is the first-time registration process?
- How do you communicate with first-time guests about what their kids experienced?
- Is your kids environment fun?

STEWARDSHIP

- Do you have other giving options (online, auto-debit)?
- Are the senior leaders implementing biblical stewardship practices (out of debt, full tithe, maximizing housing allowance, etc.)?
- Do you communicate the church's financial situation on a regular basis (in bulletin, e-newsletter, etc.)?

MINISTRY

- Do you clearly communicate expectations to volunteers (requirements, length of commitment, how to communicate, etc.)?
- Do you have places of service that are available to newcomers?
- Do you have a simple, one-step sign-up process for ministry teams?
- How consistently and creatively do senior leaders communicate their gratitude to ministry team leaders and volunteers?

- Do current volunteers and leaders do personal recruiting or do they rely entirely on stage announcements?

WEBSITE

- Are directions and service times (or a link to them) easily visible on the home page?
- Is the website updated regularly with fresh content and cleansed from old content?
- Are the graphics and layout clean and consistent with your brand?

VISION

- How often are elements of your vision communicated?
- What methods are used to communicate vision other than the stage/pulpit?
- What "sticky" word pictures or slogans have you developed to communicate vision?

LEADERSHIP DEVELOPMENT

- Do you (the lead pastor) have a written personal growth plan?
- Do you have committed and competent staff/leaders in each area of your church?
- Is every leader investing himself/herself in at least two other people in an intentional way?
- Do you have a written plan for how you identify, develop, deploy, and coach leaders in your church?

STRATEGIC

- Do you have a written, customized plan for each ministry system?
- Do you have a specific leader assigned to each ministry system?

There you have it! Now we have a lot to do, don't we? Luke has obviously been thinking about this for awhile, and he's ahead of me on these systems.

Systems don't make a great church. They don't necessarily grow your church. They don't necessarily deepen your church.

God has to work! You have to reach out and care for people. You have to preach and teach the Gospel. You have to assimilate new members and be involved in your community. Systems don't sit with people grieving in the nursing home. Systems don't send flowers or recognize birthdays.

Systems can be a way for you to get some of those tasks done and see where you need help because something is off track and broken. A system doesn't actually do anything. You do. Or someone does. You still have to fix the typos, set the meetings, type the agendas, and know what you're preaching on next week. A system serves you. You don't serve it.

Let's at least work on a few systems to see whether they will help.

Calendar

We talked about a calendar before when we discussed time. Your calendar is a map and guide for the way you both spend and value time. You have a blank slate, and you can determine what goes on your calendar. Remember that we all get done what we want to get done each day. You always have time for the important things in your life.

That's true for your church, too.

Put a time in your calendar for a few days off by yourself. When you get to that retreat, make sure you take with you that big, dry-erase calendar and some pens and get to work like we talked about. You can be getting ready for that retreat by taking notes of things you want to make sure you get on the calendar when you work on it.

So write down the key dates you know are fixed and can't be changed. Your Easter service. Your Christmas schedule. The Super Bowl. Football games if the schedule is out. NBA Thunder games are big time here in Oklahoma City. Those will be events you'll want to work around. We have a huge marathon in Oklahoma City the last Sunday morning of April that attracts 25,000 people. The route is right by our building. So that may not be the best weekend to do something important at the church like a capital campaign kickoff. I need to know that.

Now you might want to have down other key events that you need to space out like New Member's meetings. Ours happen three to four times per year, and they're really important, so I want to make sure they're on the calendar. Women's retreat. Men's retreat. Youth group summer camp.

VBS if you do it. Denominational meetings where you go out of town. Leadership retreats.

Things fill up quickly!

This is the time where you should think about when and how you want to get away. If there is a conference or retreat coming up, write it on the calendar so you can see if you have the space for it and how it lines up with other parts in the life of the church. It's a time when you can dream about some of those things you'd like to do for professional development or spiritual renewal. You're unlikely to get to that conference if you forget about it until a month ahead of time. But if it is on your calendar, you're far more likely to go. You may need to ask the finance team to approve the expense, but now it's on your radar and you look like you have a plan.

I also think this is the time to plan your sermon series. Not everyone does this. I understand that it's fairly easy if you take a long, long time to go through books of the Bible. Some of you might preach on Romans for two years. Well, then you probably don't need that much of a plan.

Others of you preach whatever you think of next. That's not a plan either, and it might work for you, but I don't think you can adequately prepare or anticipate the needs of your church that way.

In my denomination, the Presbyterian Church in America, we have a rich history of liturgy and a way of doing things. On the other hand, there is tremendous freedom. That is great, but it can also mean that we just do whatever we want without a lot of rootedness or thoughtfulness.

So my co-pastor Bobby and I decided to use a loose church calendar to order our year and work through various emphases in the church. I would love to not only mildly suggest but actually actively promote the idea of a church calendar for you, so you don't only inhabit secular time but also sacred time and bridge the gap between the two. (For just a brief thought about this, consider a few paragraphs in the subsection "The Fullness of Time" by James K. A. Smith in his book *How Not To Be Secular*, chapter one.)

Our preaching calendar at City Pres looks like this:

- Advent—the start of the church year
    - Four weeks before Christmas
    - Focus on the incarnation of Christ and what Christmas means
- Last Sunday of December—open for a guest preacher
- January to Lent
    - About six weeks
    - Focus on a short book of the Bible (like Ecclesiastes, for example)
- Lent to Easter and then Easter Sunday
    - About five weeks
    - Focus on Jesus's life and ministry, preparing for his death and resurrection
    - For example: John 12-20
    - Easter—big, big day, of course
- Easter until Pentecost
    - About six weeks
    - Focus on the church and why/how the resurrection affects daily life
    - For example: Acts 1-9, or Anchor of Hope: Why Hope Matters
    - Pentecost is a celebration of the birthday of the church

- After Pentecost all the way until the next Advent (Summer and Fall)
    - About 25ish weeks
    - This is a good time to do a long book of the Bible in one long series.
    - You can break this up into a few shorter series.
    - For example: Esther and 1, 2, 3 John or Leviticus and 1, 2 Timothy
    - We like to toggle between the Old and New Testament.
    - We like to think about issues and concerns but also not be driven by those.

You don't have to do it like this, but how do you do it? How do you decide?

So if you can think ahead, you can have every week of your year planned for what you're going to preach. Sometimes it may be fairly general, but you have a good idea that if you're doing to do nine weeks on Esther and fourteen weeks on 1, 2, 3 John, you need to space that out in the right manner so you can end the one and have time to do the other and not have to squeeze. You can know when you need a guest to help or you have a gap between two series and can preach something you've been thinking about without breaking it up.

People like to know where you're going, and you should, too. I think this also could help you do some background thinking, so you're ready to go when it is time to preach a particular series.

For example, I like to think of a theme when I preach a series. We did a series in Lent called Redeemed and Restored:

Jesus Cares for Broken People. We looked at the way he rescued people that our society would call outcasts. It was a great series. Since I knew it was coming, I was on the lookout for books about lost and broken people who had been rescued. It wasn't a huge task on my to-do list, but if I came across a book or article that seemed interesting, I'd grab it and save it for later. If I had time, I would start reading a bit so I could be thinking about it.

I found books about slavery in Africa in the early 2000s. I found articles about people who were saving abandoned babies in Korea. I used some of these, and others of them were helpful because I had in mind that there are still lost and broken and thrown-out people today. I wanted to tell those stories so my Bible text would be more alive and more real.

I could do that because I knew I'd be preaching on that and when that would be. When we were about to finish Esther and start on 1, 2, 3 John, I knew that our theme would change from God of the Details to Love. I had been reading books and articles about God's providence and about royalty because I'd been in Esther. But I needed to switch and start reading about Love. I needed to get on Amazon and troll around a bit. I needed to peruse the shelves at Barnes and Noble. This low-tech practice will often lead you to a serendipitous find. You were looking for one topic, but then you stumbled on something totally different (yet totally relevant at the same time). I need to save an article in the paper about love. I need to ask on social media about the best love movies.

That's the idea. I have it mapped out, and Bobby and I can talk about it. He knows when I'm going to be gone so he needs to preach. I know when he's going to be gone. We discuss upcoming themes and look ahead together. We share ideas and books. We make changes and updates, because the calendar is not set in stone. We can communicate with our graphic designer in time and thus get a poster made, slides to show, and something to talk about and pass out for our next series.

Our calendar helps us have a system. It helps us communicate and think and pray and plan and hopefully glorify God in what we say and do. That's what we want.

Tasks

I'm guessing you have some task management system. You have a pad of paper or notebook or an app where you record your to-do list and then mark them off as you complete them. Organized and innovative creative people also capture their ideas and thoughts in a journal or moleskin carried with them throughout the day. This was a ubiquitous practice back in the day. People called it a "commonbook." It's where ideas were recorded, and effective/creative people still make this a practice.

The classic and best resource for task completion is the aptly named *Getting Things Done* by David Allen. You should read and follow it, even if you have to modify it for it to work for you. I'm not going to talk about a classic daily to-do list. Organized people look back over their day, and they make a game plan for the next day. They think about what they have to get done. They put those things in slots and then pick the one or two most important things. They look at the list (physical or mental) and then start at it in the morning. There are resources to help you, and again I'd suggest you give up and give over to those who are more organized and more productive than you.

Your "Everything in My Brain" List

At some point as you work on your organization, you'll want to take a few hours and try to write down everything that's in your brain. Everything. That's what David Allen would have you do, and he would charge you a ton of money to stand there while you do this brain dump. You may need to take several sessions to get this out on a legal pad or Word document. You'll want to resist the urge to sort it or evaluate. You need the list to be substantiated and written down so it can stop floating around in your brain.

After you're done, you can quickly see that these ideas can be sorted. Some of them can be done in a few seconds or minutes. Why not list those together and start knocking them out? Make a list of phone calls you have to make and then make them. Send your wrong-sized shoes back. Pay the bill.

Some things are longer conversations you need to have, so you can't just complete those easily. Some are projects that involve many other steps. Some are items to pray about and take before the Lord, or ideas that may never happen. Some you're excited about. Some you're worried about. Now you can see them on the page and that your brain is firing on way more cylinders than you had thought. Your brain is full, trying to process all these things and keep them all straight. Getting those items out of your head and down on the page helps you see and sort and organize and prioritize.

When I made this list in October 2012, I had ten to twelve items pertaining to the website and graphic work we were doing for our new church. That was one of the worries I had, one of the ongoing projects that took up brain time for me. It was added to personal relationships, people in our city I wanted to contact, church members I was concerned about, fellow pastors, leadership training, my own development—and so much more.

If I made a list today (and I should), it would look totally different. Those graphic projects were completed, and now I have new ones I'm working on. People came. People left. I'm sure my list would be longer and more developed instead of shorter and completed.

You need to keep track of what you're thinking about so you can see what is in your big, huge, crazy brain. And so you can free your brain from trying to remember every detail about what needs to be done.

Things

One tool I've found the most helpful for me in being organized is Things, a program or app you buy for your computer and phone. No doubt there are others, but it's the one I started with and have kept using. (I believe it's only available for Apple products, but there are similar ones out there.)

Things can function as a traditional to-do list. However, I think it's best used if you put recurring items in the program and let the computer remember for you.

There are so many of these types of recurring items, ideas, and projects for the organized pastor to remember. Such as:

- Getting staff member reports
- Making reports
- Contacting certain people that you care about (similar to what you can do in Contactually)
- Getting the bulletin done
- Inputting certain numbers
- Submitting expense reports
- Planning recurring events
- Yearly events that come around that you need to talk about
- Ways to care for people
- Pull up and evaluate the Systems Checklist twice a year!

Let me give you a few examples and you'll get the idea.

I mentioned before that we have the Oklahoma City Memorial Marathon that happens every last Sunday of April. 25,000 people come downtown. It's an important event in our state and city, and it recognizes and commemorates the April 19, 1995, bombing of the Murrah Federal Building (that killed 168 people) and, more importantly, the hope and vision our city has for the future.

The first few years of our church, we met at 5 p.m. on Sunday nights, so it wasn't an issue for us. Then we moved to Sunday mornings when we bought our new building, and the course goes right past our building. So we now had to deal with this event and especially to communicate to everyone our plan.

The reason I'm bringing this up is because this will happen every year. It's not a one-time deal for us. So I typed up an announcement that we distributed through our communication channels.

Then I put the event and announcement in Things.

I made an entry in mid-March and set it to recur every year. I'm not thinking that I'll forget this, but you never know. I do know that it's perfect for what Things is all about and now it's off my brain and onto the computer. In the notes of the entry, I just copied and pasted the announcement itself:

> MARATHON – It's marathon Sunday coming up, and the route goes around our building. You have to approach church from the southwest corner. Get to where you can go north on Classen and turn east onto 13th. You'll need to drive around the marathon route. Downtown will be blocked and so will Classen. Allow extra and ample time. Be sensitive to neighbors for parking.

That was easy. That's what I'm talking about. It's done, and it's logged in, and it will pull up so I don't have to remember it until it's time. When it comes up on my Things, I'm ready to send out the announcement in our communications. I don't have to hunt for it or write it up new or even remember when to do it.

Just remember that when you enter in "Memorial Day Picnic," you actually need to have other entries for three months/two months/one month before that picnic so you can be getting ready for the picnic itself. I always put last year's plan and evaluation in the notes so we can have a starting place. Three months out, I make sure we're starting on the plan and then later that I'm tracking with the planners and the plan so we're ready to go when it's time.

Each year we ask for a special Christmas Offering. That is a huge process with many steps. So I have ten to twelve entries in my Things list that help guide me through it.

I have ways I want to be with my staff and volunteers. So I have entries that pop up every three to four months that will say: Ask Staff How They're Doing, Love on Staff with Words, Write Thank You Notes, Give Public Compliments, etc. When they pop up, I commit myself to try to do them.

You can make entries about topics you'd like to emphasize in your church with your blog or newsletters. January can be nursery, February—music, March—youth group, April—men's ministry, etc. It will remind you to cycle through those various emphases in your church so you don't neglect important ones because you're always distracted by the urgent ones.

I have each staff member write a simple report each week that consists of: what have you done or what are you working on, what is coming up, and how are you doing? It should take five to ten minutes. I have those entered into my Things so I know that person's report is due on that day. It reminds me if I haven't gotten it that I should ask for it. Not in a mean way. There are always reasons that a report might not get sent on the day it's due. It's no big deal if it's a day late. But if I never ask for it or follow through, then maybe the report isn't very important to me after all. I need to be able to see whether I've gotten it or not.

Things helps me. It keeps track. As I've said, I especially use it for recurring items. I have things that recur every week, every two to three weeks, every month, every three months, and just about every possible timeframe. I want to send out a

Giving Report in July each year, so I have that in Things, and then several other entries in the months preceding, so we can be preparing for that report to go out.

It's important that you also commit to clearing out your Things list. If there's an item that is due but you don't click it, you'll get desensitized to that little red notification bubble. You need to hate that red bubble that means there are unfinished items. You want a clear screen. That can be tough to achieve. But you can achieve it if you decide that you can't do that action right now and therefore it needs to go. You can achieve it tomorrow if you try to take care of it. You can also achieve it if you realize that goal or action is unrealistic and needs to be changed or its frequency needs to be adjusted and lengthened out. Make it a point and priority to get that red notification off as often as you can. Don't let it build up until you feel defeated. If that does happen, click them all, make adjustments, and start over.

As one of my seminary professors used to say, "Never stop starting." This is true for Things, and it's true in so many other areas of life like family devotions and eating healthy.

Make adjustments. Clear it out. Start over. Get organized.

There are YouTube videos about best practices for Things and ways to make it sing and hum. They'll do a far better job than I can in laying out the actual working mechanisms of the program. Invest the time in these as you get organized. Use this tool to help you, so you can spend more time doing other things you're called to do.

Money

I'd like to skip this section on money, but I can't. It's too important.

As much as many of us want this not to be true, we can't ignore it: money fuels the engine.

We're not saved by money. Good ministry doesn't happen because of money. We can do so much without any money. Money isn't Jesus. You can preach a great sermon for free. You can care for someone with an email or conversation. You can't buy me love. Money is not the answer.

But it is the fuel. Do we agree on that?

If you had 10 percent more in your budget, would you yawn? Or would you be super excited?! What if you had 20 percent more! What if you could get another $50,000? You could hire another two interns or another full-time staff. You might be able to take that class or help people on that mission trip or pay half for the playground.

You could do so much more. It would fuel more ministry.

I've raised a lot of money in my career. I started off with The Navigators. When I went on staff, we spent a week at Glen Eyrie in Colorado Springs in fundraising school with some of the masters. We talked philosophy and then practicality. We even spent a night cold calling from their *Discipleship Journal* database.

I didn't have much to raise. My first full year on staff with The Navs I made a whopping total of $16,100 (my social security statement tells me). That was in 1994. During that year I was married and had my first child. Yikes!

The policy at that time for the ministry was that if you didn't have any money in your account for the month, you didn't get paid that month. They didn't front anyone money. So if you had only raised $500, you probably received about $100 (they took out some fees). I had plenty of friends and coworkers who got checks for $100 for the month, and then try to scramble to figure out what they were going to do.

I decided that what I was going to do was figure out how to raise money!

I think I worked pretty hard at it and kept it up over the years. I tried to communicate our story and needs from all different sides and angles. I tried to talk about how great ministry was at times, but also how it was tough and exhausting. I tried to give stories about students. I tried to be creative and expressive. And I tried to honestly ask without fear.

It always took a lot of work. You never knew who would say yes. You never knew how much anyone would ever give. The most likely people wouldn't give any, and the least likely would give a little or a lot.

When I transitioned to Reformed University Fellowship at the University of Oklahoma, my budget was considerably higher. I needed to raise money for myself, my wife, and our four kids, a mortgage, and then a ministry that had an actual budget. Over the course of those ten years I spent in OURUF, I raised more than a million dollars. I kept at it. I wanted to be fully funded and never have to say no to things because I didn't have enough money. I wanted my wife Julie to have confidence that we could make it and not be always stressed and worried. I wanted to make it a part of my job that I excelled at instead of complained about.

When we agreed to start City Pres in Oklahoma City, I realized I was again signing up to raise money. We had some essential, front-loaded support from the Southwest Church Planting Network of our denomination, which made it easier to begin with confidence. But we had to ramp up quickly. A new church has some fundraising advantages over a campus ministry. But it also has some disadvantages. We needed to keep communicating and asking people to support us, even and especially people who didn't attend the church we were starting.

It all happened. We had enough. We even had more than enough and bought a building within two years of starting to worship every week. God provided, just like he always has. We raise our Ebenezer, our stone of help, our marker we set to remind ourselves that God provides so much more than we could ask or imagine. He delights to provide for his children.

Now that we have all this, I'm still a fundraiser! I always will be. It will never end. It has changed. It is different. I have more built-in opportunities for asking. I can ask for money fifty-two times a year during the worship service.

You have this ability, too, and I hope you will see yourself as always being a fundraiser. You need to be great at it. Not obsessed with it. Not seeing money in people's eyes. Not guilting them into giving more. Not treating them differently depending on their giving totals. But pastoring them and your church in one of the key areas of life.

If you're going to be effective and organized and lead your church, you need to have a mindset and plan for giving and helping to disciple people in this. Do you?

How do you track new givers? You need a system to alert you when someone has given for the first time so that person or family can receive a handwritten thank you card from you or someone on your staff.

How do you track givers who aren't giving? You need to be alerted when someone hasn't given for six months or so. You can bet something is going on. That's a pastoral concern and a trigger for at least a phone call or email. It may be something you need to know about.

What do you do to generate content for you to talk about giving? When we first started at City Pres, Bobby and I decided to hitch our wagon to the team at Giving Rocket. They did an excellent job in thinking about giving for us. Each week we'd get a Giving Talk from them that we'd use right before the offering in our service. We eventually learned how to do this ourselves, but for several years it was far easier to pay them $100 a month and do whatever they said. It was a bit like having a finance team chairman on staff for only $1200 a year. I'm sure they helped us far more than that (and if you didn't think they did, they'd give you your money back).

Do you have a State of the Union meeting where you give the numbers and set the vision for the upcoming year? Are you able to produce numbers and budgets and then speak to those in a passionate, intelligent way?

Do you have a specific and special Christmas Offering? Giving Rocket has helped with a detailed plan on how to do this, and I'd commend them to help you as well. We've been able to raise that extra $50,000 in a one-time offering on one day! This can be a massive boost to your church, its budget, and whatever projects you would like to fund. Don't miss this opportunity because you're scared and don't know how to do it. If you don't want to sign up for Giving Rocket (and they do pound you with other promotional opportunities), then ask for help from somewhere else.

I want you to succeed. I want you to have the fuel to get your ideas and programs funded.

We had a million failures. We tried to do it all ourselves the first year. One of our key men volunteered as our accountant and did a great job until he was crushed by the volume and then got far behind. We knew we needed help, so we hired an accountant and bookkeeper through DecisionGrid who now generates our reports, fixes our mistakes, and helps us stay organized. DecisionGrid produces our Profit and Loss statements and makes certain I know when we have new givers. The bookkeeper puts the names and addresses in a Google Drive file, and I erase them after I have sent a thank you card (that I purchased from Giving Rocket). DecisionGrid helps us pull data so we can send a midyear giving update letter to each church member.

We needed a system for when to collect our staff's proposed budget adjustments for the upcoming year and ways to track/report/evaluate/discuss how we're doing in reality versus the budget. We're working on those things, not because we're beholden to the budget, but because we want to be wise, intentional, responsible, responsive stewards with what God has given us and what he has in store for us.

I remind you, this isn't my cup of tea. I'm not good at this. In fact, I stink at it. I appreciate the business sense and side of it because I do like systems. I don't like bearing into all the numbers, and my eyes glaze over when I think about thousands of digits on a page.

But I want to be committed to being the most vibrant and healthy church we can be. As the lead pastor, I have to take an interest in this. I don't have to do it all, but I'm ultimately responsible for what happens, and this money thing is fuel for ministry. It's not the indicator, but it is an indicator of how things are going and how people are doing. As you evaluate your organized pastor self, how are you doing in thinking about, talking about, and helping people with money?

Where are places you can improve? Are there some churches or programs that are great at a culture of generosity that you can investigate and learn from?

What would you do if your church had more income? What dreams could you start fulfilling? What initiatives could you begin?

More More More—Because Ministry is Complicated

I could go on, but this book doesn't need to be 250 pages.

Use Luke's Systems Checklist to evaluate your systems.

The City can help you organize your church directory and communication systems.

A simple Google Drive system can help you organize documents that require collaboration. We use Google Drive to create our session meeting agendas and our bulletins, so we're all contributing to the same document and don't get an "old" copy.

Hootsuite can help you organize your social media. Or you can ask each person on your staff to make sure he or she posts on a certain day of the week. If it's on your Things list or your calendar, you can make it a point to write one thing each day. It really only takes thirty seconds—if you remember and make it a priority to just chip away at it. It doesn't have to be witty or profound or even promotional. It just needs to be there because you did something.

When do you promote, train, and restart your community groups? Do you have a system for tracking who is in them and who isn't? Do you have a system to make sure your group leaders and hosts are doing well and not burned out? Do you have a system for first-time leaders and how to evaluate how they're doing?

How will you know when the coffee cups run out or are about to? What about the communion wine and cups? What about the toilet paper? Some things are more trouble than others when you discover they're gone and empty.

Less Less Less—Because of Margins

Each day is an adventure as a pastor. There are so many things you have to take care of. It's like an entrepreneur plus. Your task is so difficult. You really do have to work hard to grow the church, network, write sermons, lead meetings, and every other thing.

In the midst of that, you will get those phone calls where everything stops.

A father comes into your office, sits down, and tells you his son is gay. What does he do?

Your buddy calls you and says he has a church member who is in the hospital in your city and would you go visit her?

You get a phone call that someone you know and love has confessed to an affair.

Your staff team is in trouble because of interpersonal conflict between two members. You have to deal with it.

This is the plus part.

You have to have an organized plan, or else you'll be up until 2 a.m. every night getting things done because you couldn't each day. You have to leave space for margin. You have to be able to know what can go, what can be delegated, and what can't be forgotten or neglected.

Your day, your week, your month, and your year need these margins for you to get done what God has for you. Many of those things are known by you. You have them down. You have them mapped out.

But some of them are unknown as of yet. You will need to change your plan and schedule in order to take care of someone—truly pastor someone—in your church or community. You'll have a funeral that is inconvenient. You'll have a trip to pick up someone at the airport who is stranded. You'll have to go and get a key made because the wedding coordinator lost it. You'll have to mop the floors because you're the one who found the leak. You'll have to drive home because your wife locked herself out. Your daughter forgot her lunch. Your youth pastor forgot the code.

Not every minute is so planned that any disruption gives you an ulcer. You have it. You're calm. You're not anxious about anything but in prayer and petition, with thanksgiving, you present your requests to God. The peace of God, which surpasses all understanding, will guard your heart and your mind in Christ Jesus.

This seems hardly possible. But it is possible. We don't have to be sitting in our offices waiting for the next terrible thing to happen. We don't have to be air traffic controllers making sure everything is under control.

But we also don't have to be scatterbrained, harried crazy people putting out fires all over the place and coming home exhausted.

We're pastors. We have an important job to do to lead the local church and to love and care for people. We hold the words of life, the words of Christ, the very words of the very person people very most need. We need to be able to hold out Christ to them, and we need to be able to grasp him ourselves.

Action Steps:

- Download the Things app or something like it. Watch some YouTube videos about how people use the apps and programs effectively.
- Plan a time to sit and get everything out of your brain and onto a file or paper. Plan a few more of those times.
- Look over Luke's Systems Checklist and make a few appointments to work through some of the items. Enter Luke's Checklist into your Things so it comes up every six to nine months. Include the checklist in the notes section in that entry.
- Work on your Things app so you don't download it and then ignore it.
- Get a planning retreat on your calendar and assemble everything you'll need for it.
- Plan out your year and get it all down. See how that feels.
- Sign up for Giving Rocket, at least for a free first month.
- Learn how to be a great fundraiser.
- Read *Ask Without Fear* at fundraisingcoach.com.
- Read *Funded and Free* at fundedandfree.com.
- Consider the margins in your day and how you could add more if needed.
- Pray. Ask God to give you freedom and take away your anxiety. Ask to trust him more. Make a Worry List, where you write down the things that are keeping you from this freedom and trust.

Chapter 4

You

One of my favorite television shows is *Restaurant Impossible* on the Food Network. If you haven't watched it, you should because it's really about life. It's certainly about leadership and pastoring.

Robert Irvine shows up at a failing restaurant. They've asked him to come to save it. He has two days and $10,000 to assess the reasons they're unsuccessful and then get it all straightened out and back on track.

Robert always reworks the menu. He always hates the food. He always redesigns the inside of the restaurant. He always talks to people about why they don't come to visit the restaurant or why they've stopped coming. He always goes into a tizzy or a frenzy or has an emotional moment. He deals with dirty kitchens, overhyped expectations, and sassy serve crews. He deals with lazy workers and checked-out employees. Everyone has excuses.

But the biggest problem always is—do you know what it is?

It's the owners.

The owners can't get it right. They won't lead. They shift the blame. They don't know costs or how to track them. No one has told them how to set their prices or manage their staff. They're in over their heads. They can't or won't taste the food. They're holding onto traditions that don't work anymore. They don't clean. They don't take time off. They're exhausted. They're defensive. They fight.

And the restaurant is failing. That's why they called Robert in the first place. They want help, but they want him to come in and blame everyone else. They are always hoping for a few quick fixes. Have they seen the show?! Don't they know this is going to be a big, big ordeal?

You may not be in that situation in your life or in your church. Things may not be quite that bad. You really may need a few tweaks. You may not have passed the crazy, failing standard that it might take for you to show up on *Pastor Impossible*, if there were such a show.

When I talk to pastors, I'm certainly not Robert Irvine. I don't wield a sledgehammer, I don't have that sort of authority, and I'm definitely not that cool.

However, when I speak with pastors who have asked me for help, I hear a ton of blame-shifting. It makes sense to me why. It's always someone else's fault. The website management. The property. The finances. The staff team. The dynamics. The visitors. The denomination. The preaching. The volunteers.

I get it. I'm there. I've been there, and I'm still there. I can't stand the weeds in our church's flowerbed, and I've asked them to be pulled and killed. They're still there! I need a few things to make this happen. I need to take ownership, and then if it's important I need to make sure it happens. Or I need to do it myself. And I need a system so that we can get the weeds out of there and have them stay out. I need that to be a value in our church and for our staff—that little things matter, too. It's how we present ourselves and a way we say we care. If we can't keep weeds out, we need to remove that as a value, or I need to figure out who can do a better job of making sure it happens, or I need to get rid of that flower bed.

What I'm suggesting is that change starts with ME. In your church it starts with YOU. I know you can't control and change every dynamic in your church. There are pressures piling on you that you can't ever seem to fix. Some you inherited. Some you created. Some no one can ever know about except you. You carry it alone with Jesus.

So let's change what you can change. It can start with your schedule and getting a handle on it. This can mean taking a true day off. It can mean working on organizing your week, your month, your year so that you can do the best job you can without giving up or giving in. It's the things we've been talking about and working on through this book. You are the owner of the restaurant. It's not impossible! But you have to agree that you are the most important part of that equation.

Ask God to help you. See that you need help. I'm not just telling you that you need to do better and pull yourself up by the bootstraps. I want you to agree that you can't do it.

That's why you need help. That may be why you picked up this book. It's okay to need help. We all do. That's what grace is all about. Now let's keep going forward.

Getting Help—A Coach

I was sitting in the coffee shop as I often do, probably sending emails and thinking about writing a sermon. I had seen this man many times. He knew people I knew. We had made eye contact, but I hadn't met him yet. I usually try to meet the regulars in the coffee shop, but I don't want to stalk them.

But I had to talk to him. Had to. Why? Every time he opened his laptop, I saw the sticker he'd put on it. It said, "I Mentor Leaders."

I googled it, found his website and checked him out online.

His name was Michael Smith, and everyone called him Smitty. He'd been a successful businessman, but now spent time with leaders to help them be the most effective they could be. His website was personable, and it resonated with me.

I went up to him and his latte that day. I introduced myself and asked if I could sit down. I nodded to his laptop sticker and said, "I'm a leader. Would you mentor me?"

He didn't say yes right away, but eventually he did. We started meeting together every other week for a few hours. He hadn't mentored a pastor before, so some of what he said took some translating out of business and into my world. But he really cared about me. He really cared about City Pres. He cared about Bobby and started meeting with him, too. He cared about my wife and family.

One thing I appreciated most about Smitty was that he was in for helping me, no holds barred. He didn't worry about upsetting me, which he often did. He didn't care about the denominational politics, though he learned about them. He asked questions as an outsider, and he didn't walk on eggshells. He called my bs when he saw it. I had to admit failures to him that other people hadn't seen.

He helped me see and institute structures and systems that weren't just true in leading an organization—they were true for life. He's the one who taught me about Things. He tried to press me into Evernote (but I like Google Drive better). He's helped me track what I think is most important. He's introduced me to key people who can help me where he can't. He's come to services and events in our church because he believes in me and us and wants us to succeed. Likewise, I've introduced him to pastors who need his help. And so many do!

I'm thankful for Smitty and how he's helped me. He's helped me be a much better pastor and taught me things I didn't learn in seminary and hadn't learned by experience yet.

I also want to tell you about Jason Economides, who I originally met through a Contactually webinar. Jason did a bang-up presentation, which you can find on the Contactually website, and at the end he extended an offer for a few free consultations.

I won't always jump on that, but I sometimes will. If I feel like I can get some help, then I'll ask for it. I didn't want to waste his time or mine, but I figured I wouldn't know unless I tried. Since I knew I had the freedom to bow out, I decided to give it a go.

I called Jason, and we talked for several hours about City Pres. Like anyone who is good at what he does, Jason listened to me about what I was doing and what challenges to success I was facing. At the end, he gave me some practical advice that proved very helpful.

He also asked me something else; he asked if we could keep meeting together. He said he enjoyed working with me and also wanted to do something to help the church succeed. He felt like he was helping someone and something with a higher purpose and that was an effort he wanted to be involved in. So I said yes!

Jason lives in Geneva, Switzerland, so he'd stay up late on our phone call evenings so we could meet at 2 p.m. my time. We talked a lot in the weeks and months leading up to our church's Easter launch. He has a keen eye for marketing materials and for catching people's attention. I realized I tended to be fairly boring and long-winded in my marketing when I started explaining things. Jason helped me with that.

His organization and business has a treasure trove of materials to help businesses grow. Some of the materials won't work for you, but they'll spark other ideas you can pursue to get you where you need to be to grow and deepen your church.

Both Smitty and Jason are coaches who have helped me immensely. They stand out to me because both have been more intentional and less occasional than my usual informal help. I've had to sign up and make a commitment. I've had to pay money. I've had to break appointments if I couldn't come. Something was on the line.

I've benefited from informal coaches, though, too.

Bobby and I drove to Memphis to meet with Jeffrey and Jeremy to talk about church planting. We asked for brochures and information packets as we assembled ours. We surveyed various pastors to help us determine the best way to create our leadership training program. We always try to pick the brains of people around us and especially those with whom we resonate.

When we worked on our capital campaign, Todd McMichen with Auxano coached us through it. We didn't just execute his plan; he helped us understand how to develop and then implement a plan. It was glorious.

You need coaching. It's worth spending time and money to get it. Don't be too picky on the front end. Get an idea and then start. You can always change course. You can always find someone different, but you need to have input into your life from someone who cares about you and wants to help you succeed, without worrying every second about your position and status as pastor.

You can supplement this coaching with intentional reading. I think reading both business-minded and idea-making books are important in your development for being an organized pastor. You don't have to be a business to learn from business resources. You can capture some ideas and principles and then translate them into your context and situation.

You can be coached and mentored from books like:

- All of Jim Collins's books, especially *Great By Choice*
- *Creativity, Inc.*, by Ed Catmull and Amy Wallace
- *Where Good Ideas Come From*, by Steven Johnson
- *Disney U*, by Doug Lipp
- *The Advantage*, by Patrick Lencioni and anything else by him

- *The Emotionally Healthy Church,* by Peter Scazzero
- *Start With Why*, Simon Sinek
- *Leading With a Limp*, Dan Allender
- *The Leadership Challenge*, Kouzes and Posner
- *Church Unique*, Will Mancini

Since I'm mentioning books and reading, I strongly encourage you to read outside of your specific specialties. Create stacks of books on topics that interest you—just because. Not everything has to be intentional all the time. Read biographies from people and time periods that fascinate you. Go on rabbit trails. Don't be so serious. Read poetry and fiction to mix things up.

For coaching and mentoring, there are also programs you can look into. You might consider a Doctor of Ministry, or you might enroll in a business degree at the university closest to you. This may also be a fantastic place for networking and meeting like-minded people in your city. Sign up for your city's leadership program. I'll bet they have one and would love to have you.

Keep learning! Take the time. Pay the cost. Ask for help and give yourself over to it. Put time, money, and energy into yourself, and it will pay off as an investment in the future of your church, pastoring, and ministry.

Getting Clarity—The Heart

While you're at it, you should spend some time on you. An organized pastor is one who is getting to know himself or herself, too. You've been working on clearing up your life. You're trying to get more organized and responsible. You're taking ownership of what it is that you've been blaming others for. You're seeing holes and needs that you vaguely knew about but had pushed down. You're investing in systems, time away, and programs to help you leap forward in what it is God wants you to do.

How are you doing?

As you clear out the debris, you may find out something unsettling: you don't like what you find in there. It's true. Your busyness and your crazy living may have been the perfect mask for not only an unsettled month, but in fact an unsettled heart.

Don't be surprised by this. We all have unsettled hearts. In fact, there may be things that need to be disturbed so that you can better love God and others.

As you work on organization and effectiveness, I want to encourage you that you also must rest in Christ. We'll talk about some specific ways to go about resting and some reasons for rest, but before we do I hope you'll see and know and agree that we're going after something deeper.

We want to be at rest with God. We want to be well thought of by him. We want to be cherished. We want to be loved and esteemed. We want to be forgiven.

When I clear away the excuses and admit that the busyness has served as a mask, I may be surprised to find:

- Defensiveness
- Addictions
- Anger
- Resentment
- Entitlement
- Overwork and underwork
- A lack of boundaries

- Hiding sin so I don't have to confess it
- Pulling back from people out of fear
- Fear!
- Confusion
- Doubt
- Unfaithfulness
- Overeating
- Obsessions
- Hatred
- Laziness

And I'm sure there are others. I often think about what the authors of the Westminster Larger Catechism were discussing when they wrote the extensive lists about what is prohibited in the Ten Commandments. They listed things I never would have thought to be implied in the first commandment.

When I consider my own heart and my own needs, I can't stop at organization. I can't think that if I conquer this, I have now dominated the world and I'll be good to go.

The truth is, I need counseling! I'm in trouble. It's a dangerous world, and as Paul Tripp says, it's a Dangerous Calling. In fact, I'm a dangerous person. I'm living in a dangerous time. I have been given dangerous responsibilities and relationships to steward. I probably can't handle it.

Take a deep breath.

We don't have to fix everything this second, and it's unlikely we'll ever get fixed. But we can make progress and we can see change.

As Rev. Tim Keller puts it, the bad news is we're worse off than we ever thought. But the good news is that Christ loves us and pays for us more than we ever thought!

As I work on loving people better, I'm going to have to take stock of more than my calendar and Things app. Contactually isn't going to help.

I'm going to have to work on my heart. I'll have to be more able to tell my story with clarity, humility, and hope. I'm going to need to know my personality profile and how it interacts with the world. I'm going to need to consider my birth order and place in the family and how that affects the way I go through life. I'm going to need to talk about key events in my story that I have either never processed or need to process more, so I can see the complex connections that these make in my worldview and outlook.

I'm going to need to examine my heart and confess not just the easy sins (what author Jerry Bridges calls Respectable Sins), but also the deep, tough, uncomfortable, ongoing ones. I'm going to need to see how I have wrongly interacted with and viewed my body, eating, thinking, emotions, sex, money, power, position, and status—and how these things aren't all just fine and at perfect peace in my life. I'm going to have to admit I've damaged other people with my words, actions, and performance, even when it was unintentional.

Seeing and working on these things doesn't mean blabbing all of them to everyone or blogging about your shortcomings every day. It probably will mean a lot of tears and crying out to God. And actual crying. It will probably mean seeing a counselor yourself instead of just being a counselor to everyone else. It will mean having to admit you are angry, not just that you were angry.

Getting Rest—The Gospel Is for You, Too

I don't know many lazy pastors. I do know disorganized ones, but they're not lazy. They don't goof off. They work hard. You work hard. You care about people. You give your life away. You bear the brunt of pain and suffering, and you rarely get the credit you deserve.

You also have your own pain and suffering. Some of your disorganization and your busyness is to hide this hurt away. When you give it space, it can threaten to undo you.

The Gospel is for you, too. It's not just for them. It's not just for your church, your people, your networks, your city. It's for you. God loves you in Christ. He loves you.

You need rest. Your soul needs rest. You can't go a mile a minute caring for everyone else. You have to stop and really, really sit in the truth that God loves you. He's forgiven you. You are good enough. You are fine. You are cherished. You are loved.

It's so easy to forget, isn't it?

I love to work. I pass this off and brush it aside. OCD people get more done! They come home from pastoring and then have hours and hours of computer time to tinker with programs, email people, and investigate new ways of doing things.

Church planting is stressful. I had to gather money, people, resources, and momentum. I had to talk people into trusting me. I had to convince them that I knew what I was talking about, so they'd show up at meetings and worship, they'd give their time and money, and they'd invite others to do the same. There were dynamics at play with other churches and pastors. The people we were gathering had their own massive problems we started to deal with. We moved. Our kids were disoriented. I had my own issues with my wife and kids, with friendships, and money. I had my own disrupted heart as I felt unsure of myself or too sure of myself.

It was a bad place.

You may be in that place, or you may have been in that place. Or you may get in that place soon enough.

You need help. You need to give up. You need to admit you need grace. You can talk to someone. You can reach out. You can get away. You can make space. You can hear God. You can be forgiven and loved.

Your heart needs rest.

In the midst of this really tough time for me, pastor Sam Storms spent time with me. He kept impressing on me the same things you can read in his book *The Singing God*. Zephaniah 3:17 says, *"The Lord your God is in your midst,*

a mighty one who will save;

he will rejoice over you with gladness;

he will quiet you by his love;

he will exult over you with loud singing."

I'm a pastor, and I preach the Gospel—and I forget this!

In the midst of emails, budgets, counseling, peacemakers, confessions, liturgies, I forget that God loves me, cares for me, watches over me, makes intercession for me. To paraphrase John Newton, I forget to love and sing and wonder, because I forget that he has hushed the Law's loud thunder.

I want to be organized and effective. But I must remember to rest in the fact that I am loved. The Gospel is for me. It's for you. We don't just hold out the word of life; it is for us! We don't just disperse the body and blood of Christ; it is for us!

We come to it by faith. We don't deserve it, but we must have it. It's a mystery for us, too. God needs to be, has to be, at work in our lives. We hold these things. We talk about them. We swim in them and wrestle with them. We must grasp them and let them into our minds, hearts, and lives. We must be affected. We must be transformed. We must be tender people who know we are deeply loved. We have to share our poverty because it's only in our foolishness that Christ is made strong. It's not our strength, our might, our wisdom, our riches, but only God's that we proclaim.

We can't be good enough to earn his favor, but neither are we too lost, too busy, too sneaky to forfeit his love. He loves even his pastors, no matter how big or small their churches, no matter how big or small their hearts and brains. No matter how full their schedules or how proficient their systems.

He loves you.

Rest in him.

Carve out that time.

Hopefully you can rest well during your weekly day off. It's tough. It feels so unnatural, but it is important. When I take off on Fridays, I have to leave my computer at home. If I take it with me, I'll work. I also have to leave home! If I stay home, I'll work.

It's still a challenge for me to figure out what I can do that's not at home and without my computer. Sometimes I get a massage—it's hard to work while getting a massage. This also helps with stress. I like to eat at different restaurants by myself and take a novel with me. I will often then go to a movie. I never used to go to movies by myself, but now I do all the time. I'll see almost whatever is playing at two or three in the afternoon, and if it stinks, oh well. Or I'll do something in the city I've always wanted to do or take a nap. Then I go work out at the gym and go home.

Taking Fridays off means I can't make appointments on Fridays. It's tough to say no to people, and every once in awhile I say yes (when someone needs to get let into the building to fix the air conditioner, I'm there!). I try to say no and do say no and figure out a different time. People usually don't mind.

It also means I must have my sermon done on Thursday (I admit that I work on my pulpit notes on Saturday morning). It means some things have to get scrunched during the week. It means I need to save my errands and housework days for Saturday and not make Fridays a work day in that sense.

It's not a Sabbath in the technical, biblical sense because it's not on the correct day of the week, and it doesn't involve worship with God's people. But it's that day of rest that I need because I'm working on the Sabbath. Just like in the Bible and just like what was always true, this day of rest takes faith. It's not easy. It doesn't seem like a good idea.

It wasn't like a day of rest was easy back in 1000 BC either. People needed to work. They had to work. Think about life without refrigerators or any types of motors. Think about how much time it would take to thresh the grain and tend the fields. There had to always be more to do. They probably weren't obsessed about free time like we are, because they were always working.

Yet God had a mandatory day where—by faith—they had to rest and worship. We need these boundaries. We need these day-markers so we can test our hearts and see whether we are able to give up the idolatries that we so easily pass off as godly when in fact they're killing our souls.

Try it. Take that day by faith. Rest. Rest in Christ in grace by faith. Give him your church and its people. Give him your city. Give him your very heart and then sit in some of the discomfort as you think of all the things that aren't getting done because you are taking time for restorative activities (or inactivities).

Jesus loves your church more than you do. He is rejoicing over you with gladness. He is the one who is mighty to save. It's not all up to you. He is the head of the church—of your church. He loves your people. He loves the lost. He is at work.

Pick up a book to read to take with you. Not for sermon preparation. Read *The Valley of Vision* prayers. Read Henri Nouwen or Eugene Peterson and journal your thoughts. Read Christian Wiman's essays in *My Bright Abyss*.

Go on a prayer walk. Pray long prayers. Pray one hundred short prayers.

Go for a long drive or a long run. Get away. Go sit in a state park and don't tell anyone where you're going. Book yourself that night in a hotel room or at a monastery and spend the time in silence.

Be ready for your Sunday by being as prepared as you can be. I hope some of this organization will help you walk into Sunday with more confidence that God has spoken to you throughout the week.

Be ready because you have spent time with God. You've taken your burdens to God. You've seen him answer prayers. You've spent time in the Bible. You are crying out like David in your own psalms as you read and relate to his cries of anguish, need for help, and promised provision.

May worship on Sunday be authentic and true to you as you sing, "Lord I need you, every hour I need you." As you confess the Nicene Creed to be true. As you tell stories of a still-rescuing God. As you invite people to know a God who is still at work, even in the least likely places, even in the here and now, but yet in such ancient, always rooted ways.

May you find rest for your own soul as you know that—in Christ alone—you are loved. You are free. You can mess it all up. You can be disorganized and loved. You can say the wrong thing, lead the wrong way, make everyone mad and lose it all —and you are loved.

Jesus is enough. I'm not sure I always believe that. But I want to.

Most of the time I believe it's Jesus + never missing an appointment ever again. Or + Things. Or Jesus + Anything! Something! The crazy thing is that Jesus knows this. He forgives even that. He still walks with me in my ADHD, my guilt and shame, and my wayward unfaithfulness.

Jesus is patient and kind. He is just and takes the blame and penalty. He gives us his life as we give him our sin. He gives us a hope for a future forever with him.

I know I've gotten past organization, and you didn't sign up for all of that. This is supposed to be a practical book, and I've tried to keep it practical for you.

However, at the foundation of it all is the truth and reality, the mystery and hope of Christ. We're supposed to do all we can to glorify God and enjoy him forever. I believe that. That's our chief end and the chief end of everything.

What's the chief end of organization? To glorify God and enjoy him forever.

What's the chief end of excellent communication, reading lists, and days off? To glorify God and enjoy him forever.

We get so off track. I'm the chief offender, not the one who is doing this perfectly. I'm at fault. I have a thousand excuses. I make mistakes over and over even when I know better. I get depressed, overwhelmed, upset, critical. I get over-zealous and charge ahead too quickly and boldly.

I need Jesus more than I need to be organized. I need Jesus more than I need anything. I need to know him and enter into his love for me, a love that I don't fully understand by any stretch. But it's true. When you get clearer in your heart, I hope you will see more clearly God's love for you in Christ and your need and desire for him. I pray that you will rest in him all the more, never less.

For me and for you as pastors and as people, as beloved sons and daughters of Jesus Christ, the King of Kings and Lord of Lords, the Redeemer of God's elect, the Victor, the Hero, the Alpha and the Omega, the Lamb of God who was slain for the world, the Author and Perfector, the Way, the Truth, and the Life. May we find ourselves ever more fully in him.

Action Steps:

- Get help! It may be a church planting coach or a leadership coach. Consider Smitty at theDecisionGrid.com or Jason at Eco Business Academy. Contact a DMin program near you or search for leadership coaches in your area.
- Consider seeing a counselor who can help you love God and others more fully.
- Have true friendships with people who know you and will walk with you.
- Set up your own mastermind group that meets each month. You can easily read a few books and research how to do this.
- Take a day off each week. Figure out what gives you rest and keeps you from sneaking in work.
- Get your yearly vacation on the calendar and hopefully some study days for you to get away.
- Buy and read some devotional books or biographies that aren't sermon prep.
- Make an Indelible Grace station on Pandora and listen to retuned hymns.
- Memorize Zephaniah 3:17.
- Hang a piece of art in your office to remind you that God loves you.
- Preach the Gospel to yourself every day.

More? Oh, There's More!

Maybe some other time we could talk about:

- Your preaching
- How you treat volunteers and staff
- How to create vision and momentum
- The importance of great parties
- The Cardinals Way
- Communication excellence and diligence
- Phases in your church
- The tension place of similarity and dissimilarity
- How people make decisions
- ROI
- Building community
- Small groups and community groups
- Creating a space
- The ancient church for a real present today
- Partnering with others in your city
- Leadership principles
- Your family

About the Author

Doug Serven is a pastor at City Presbyterian Church in Oklahoma City. Doug grew up in southwest Missouri and graduated with a journalism degree from the University of Missouri-Columbia. He worked for The Navigators for four years, including three at Oklahoma State University, before going to Covenant Theological Seminary, where he earned an MDiv. Doug then moved to Oklahoma to begin ordained pastoral campus work with Reformed University Fellowship at the University of Oklahoma. He and his wife, Julie, and their four kids moved to Oklahoma City in 2011 to start City Pres.

Made in the USA
Middletown, DE
06 June 2019